The Modern World
Themes in Twentieth-Century World History

Chris Jordan

Queen Elizabeth's School and Community College, Crediton

Tim Wood

John Murray

HISTORY IN ACTION   Chris Jordan and Tim Wood

Already published (for lower secondary):
England in the Middle Ages
The Ancient World
Old World, New World: 1480–1600

In preparation:
The Invaders

Acknowledgements

The authors and publishers are grateful to the following for permission to reproduce copyright material:

Associated Press pages 12A, 65 (8), 92A; BBC Hulton Picture Library pages 13B, 29G, 37D, 53D 67I, 80, 81A, C, E, 82 (centre top), 91B; Bildarchiv Preussischer Kulturbesitz page 60 (top); Gunn Brinson Collection pages 36A, 43H; Bundesarchiv pages 46 (left and bottom right), 75; Rene Burri/Magnum page 51D; Camera Press pages 51 (top), 52A, 56; Ernest Cole/John Hillelson Agency pages 78 (bottom right and top left); Crown Copyright reserved page 71 (bottom); Mary Evans Picture Library pages 34, 40B, 74; Ronald Gray *Hitler and the Germans* (1981) pages 40A, 45C; Robert Harding Picture Library pages 86, (All) 87 (All); Illustrated London News Picture Library page 59 (top); Trustees of the Imperial War Museum 5B, C, E, 9F, G, 45B, 62 (left and centre), 64 (3) (5), 65 (7) (9), 69D; International Institute of Social History page 36B; The Keystone Collection 11, 14, 18, 19E, 35 (both), 37E 41C, 50, 59 (bottom), 61 (top) 78 (centre right), 82, (top, centre right and centre left), 88, (top) 91C, 93 (both); W.S.M. Knight *The History of the Great European War*; G.S. Lidstone *On Guard* (1945) pages 66, 67D, E, H; Moro Roma page 4 (bottom); Alain Nogues/John Hillelson Agency page 78 (bottom left); Novosti Press Agency pages 22C, 23D, 28B, D, 29H, 77; Popperfoto pages 61 (bottom), 88 (bottom); *Punch* pages 15, 17B; Religious Society of Friends page 53 (bottom); Society for Anglo-Chinese Understanding pages 48, 49, 52B, 55, 57 (top and bottom); Solo Syndications pages 16A, 33C, 63; P.F. Speed *A Course Book in Modern World History* (1982) page 60 (bottom); Suddeutscher Verlag pages 38, 46 (top right), 82 (bottom), 91A; Topham Picture Library page 64 (2), 84; Ullstein Bilderdienst pages 39, 42A, B.

Grateful thanks to Linda Taylor for her help with picture research, and to Paddy Storrie of St Joan of Arc's School, Rickmansworth, for ideas used in Unit 2.

Every effort has been made to contact copyright holders. We will be pleased to rectify any omissions in future printings.

First published 1989
by John Murray (Publishers) Ltd
50 Albemarle Street, London W1X 4BD

British Library Cataloguing in Publication Data

Jordan, Chris, *1952–*
 The modern world : themes in twentieth
 century world history.
 1. World, 1900–
 I. Title II. Wood, Tim
 909.82

 ISBN 0–7195–4529–3
 (Teachers' book ISBN 0–7195–4530–7)

Designed by Tony Stocks
Layout by John Hawkins
Diagrams by Ian Foulis
Illustrations by Philip Page

Typeset by Chapterhouse, Formby L37 3PX

Printed and bound in Great Britain at The Bath Press, Avon

CONTENTS

PROPAGANDA

It is 1916. The Great War has been going on for two years. Millions of men have been killed. Hundreds of thousands of them are British.

Instructions

Study all the sources on these two pages. Read all the questions following the evidence before writing any answers.

The German Emperor.

How one newspaper sees the Kaiser.

SOURCE A

Recruiting posters

SOURCE B

SOURCE C

Questions

Look carefully at Sources A–E.

1 What impression of the Germans do the sources give you?

2 What impression of the British do the sources give you?

3 Are these impressions entirely truthful? Explain your answer.

4 What do you think was the attitude of British people to men who refused to join the army?

5 Do you think this material accurately shows the attitude of Britons to the war in 1916? Explain your answer.

Reports of evil deeds done by the Germans

SOURCE D

SOURCE E

WHAT A RED RAG IS TO A BULL-

THE RED CROSS IS TO THE HUN.

To the already Long List of Outrages by the HUNS on The RED CROSS both on Land and Sea, there was added on January the 4th This Year, the Sinking without warning in the Bristol Channel of the Hospital Ship "REWA,"—Fortunately owing to the Splendid Discipline and the Unselfish and Heroic Conduct of the Officers, Crew, and The Medical Staff, All the wounded, of whom there were over 700 on board were saved,—But three poor Lascar Firemen went down with the ship.

CONCHIES

1 What method had the British army used to get soldiers to join up before 1916?

2 What change took place in March 1916?

3 Write a report on each of the witnesses described in **Resource A** (maximum 400 words each), explaining:
(a) a little of their background;
(b) why they applied for Certificates of Exemption;
(c) the Tribunal's decision;
(d) what you think will happen to them in the next few weeks.

It is 1916. The people of Britain have no doubt that the Great War is a just war. People are convinced that the Germans are inhuman and uncivilised.

Before 1916

The British army was a *volunteer army*. Over a million men had come forward eagerly to join up. However, the casualties were so high that many more men were needed. The government decided to introduce *military conscription*.

The government realised that a huge effort would be needed to win the war. If more men went into the army, women would have to replace them in factories to produce weapons, or on farms to produce food.

The German U-boat campaign was causing shortages of everything so everyone in Britain was suffering. German Zeppelins had bombed London, killing women and children. This had never happened before.

The government wanted two and a half million men to join the armed forces.

The notices on these two pages show the kind of pressure put on men by the government just before conscription was introduced.

1. Have you any fit men between the ages of 18 and 36 years of age serving behind your counter who at this moment ought to be serving their country?

2. Will you call your male employees together and explain to them that in order to end the war quickly we must have more men?

3. Will you tell them what you are prepared to do for them while they are fighting for the Empire?

4. Have you realised that we cannot have 'business as usual' whilst the war continues?

THE ARMY WANTS MORE MEN TODAY

5. Could not Women or older men fill their places till the war is over?

YOUR COUNTRY WILL APPRECIATE THE HELP YOU GIVE.

God Save the King

Military Service Act 1916

On 2 March 1916 the Military Service Act came into force. This made it *compulsory* for men of military age to join the armed forces.

Men who wanted to be exempt (excused) from being conscripted (made to join up) had to appear in front of a *Military Tribunal* to give their reasons. If their reasons were thought to be good enough they could get a *Certificate of Exemption*.

Military Service Act, 1916

Every man to whom the act applies will be taken to have enlisted for the period of the war unless he is exempt.

Any man who has adequate grounds for applying for a Certificate of Exemption should do so at once.

Why wait for the act to apply to you? Come now and join of your own free will. You can at once put your claim before a Local Tribunal for exemption from being called up for military service if you wish.

APPLY NOW

The Military Tribunal interviewed the candidates to see what their reasons were. People could be excused war service if they could show that they had genuine reasons of conscience for not wanting to fight. These people were called *conscientious objectors* (people who objected to fighting for reasons of conscience). They were nicknamed '*conchies*'.

Conscientious objectors could only get a certificate if they had a genuine reason for not joining up. It was the job of the Tribunal to make sure that the reasons were genuine. Once the conchies had been interviewed, the Tribunal decided what was to be done with them.

Military age

At first all unmarried men between the ages of 19 and 38 were eligible for conscription. By the summer of 1916, this had been extended to include married men up to the age of 41.

Instructions

You are the Military Tribunal. It is the summer of 1916. You have to interview four people who have applied for exemption from the Military Service Act. All of them are eligible to be conscripted.

You must question them to decide if they have genuine reasons of conscience. You can also excuse them if their present job is vital for the war effort and they cannot be replaced by an older man or a woman.

Remember hundreds of thousands of our young men have died for their country. Almost everyone in Britain has lost a son, a husband, a father or a friend. All the time you are interviewing them, *think* – are they genuine conscientious objectors or are they cowards trying to wriggle out of serving their country?

Questions

4 You may not have agreed with some of the decisions. Explain any differences you may have had with the Tribunal.

5 Do you think treatment of conscientious objectors in 1916 was fair? Explain your answer.

Sentencing Conchies

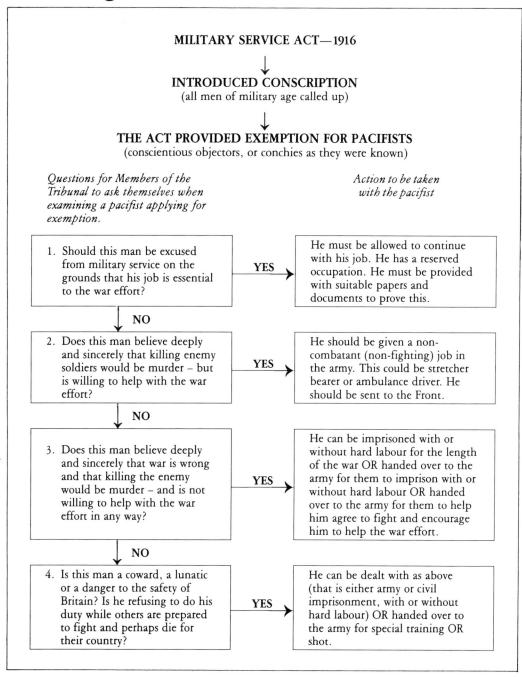

MILITARY SERVICE ACT—1916

↓

INTRODUCED CONSCRIPTION
(all men of military age called up)

↓

THE ACT PROVIDED EXEMPTION FOR PACIFISTS
(conscientious objectors, or conchies as they were known)

Questions for Members of the Tribunal to ask themselves when examining a pacifist applying for exemption.

Action to be taken with the pacifist

1. Should this man be excused from military service on the grounds that his job is essential to the war effort? — **YES** → He must be allowed to continue with his job. He has a reserved occupation. He must be provided with suitable papers and documents to prove this.

NO ↓

2. Does this man believe deeply and sincerely that killing enemy soldiers would be murder – but is willing to help with the war effort? — **YES** → He should be given a non-combatant (non-fighting) job in the army. This could be stretcher bearer or ambulance driver. He should be sent to the Front.

NO ↓

3. Does this man believe deeply and sincerely that war is wrong and that killing the enemy would be murder – and is not willing to help with the war effort in any way? — **YES** → He can be imprisoned with or without hard labour for the length of the war OR handed over to the army for them to imprison with or without hard labour OR handed over to the army for them to help him agree to fight and encourage him to help the war effort.

NO ↓

4. Is this man a coward, a lunatic or a danger to the safety of Britain? Is he refusing to do his duty while others are prepared to fight and perhaps die for their country? — **YES** → He can be dealt with as above (that is either army or civil imprisonment, with or without hard labour) OR handed over to the army for special training OR shot.

7

THE FATE OF THE CONCHIES

Questions

1 What were considered 'genuine reasons of conscience' for which men could be granted Certificates of Exemption?

2 Describe the treatment of conscientious objectors in prison.

3 Source C describes the methods used by the army to make John Gray obey orders. Why was the army so keen to get conscientious objectors to obey even one order?

4 Look at Source E. What is the attitude of the soldiers to the conscientious objectors? Why do the soldiers have a different opinion from civilians in 1916?

The tribunal you held may have been quite tough on the conchies you questioned. In 1916, Military Tribunals were very tough indeed. 6261 conscientious objectors were arrested and imprisoned. Of these, 71 died in prison; 31 went mad; all had a very rough time. Read the written reports about the treatment of five conscientious objectors and then answer the questions.

SOURCE A

The conscientious objector . . . seemed to most people to be merely a shirker (someone who avoided their responsibilities) . . . The women he knew cut his acquaintance (ignored him), his mother and his brothers often jeered at him at home. Shirker, coward, dog were the words they were thought to deserve.

John Graham, a Quaker leader.

SOURCE B

We were tied by the wrists to horizontal ropes about five feet (1.5 m) off the ground with our arms outstretched and our feet tied together. There were 11 of us in a cell 12 feet by 12 feet (4 m²).

Howard Marten, put into military prison by the army.

SOURCE C

The bombing officer threw a live Mill's bomb at his feet after removing the pin . . . he failed to persuade Gray to throw it. Gray stood perfectly still and calm when the bomb was hissing at his feet and the officer who threw it had to run for cover . . . He was stripped naked, a rope tightly fastened round his stomach and he was pushed forcibly and entirely immersed (ducked) in a filthy pond in the camp grounds eight or nine times in succession and dragged out each time by the rope. The pond contained sewage . . . (Gray eventually gave in and obeyed the orders given to him.)

John Gray, put into the army for 'special training' to make him obey orders.

SOURCE D

I was bullied horribly when I was tried and sentenced to 28 days solitary confinement . . . the confinement was in a pit ten feet (3 m) deep. The bottom is full of water and I have to stand on two strips of wood all day long just above the waterline. There is no room to walk about and sitting is impossible. The sun beats down and all through the long day there are only walls of clay to look at. Already I am half mad . . . within a few days I will be sent to France and shot like a dog for disobedience . . .

From a letter smuggled out of an army camp hidden in a cigarette packet.

SOURCE E

It was right at the beginning that I learnt that the only people from whom I could expect sympathy were the soldiers and not the civilians . . . I was waiting in the guardroom when five soldiers under arrest came in. When they asked me what I was in for I was as simple as possible – 'I am a Quaker and I refused to join the army because I think that war is murder'. 'Murder?' one of them whispered. 'Murder? It's bloody murder.' As they went away they each came up to me and shook me by the hand – 'Stick to it matey,' they said, one after another.

The report of a Quaker conchie.

SOURCE F

AN "OBJECT" LESSON

PLATE 9.

—By permission of John Bull

"This little pig stayed at home"

SOURCE G

GO!
IT'S YOUR
DUTY LAD
JOIN TO-DAY

Questions

5 Source F is a piece of propaganda. Explain what its purpose is. How does the artist show the conscientious objector? Do you think it is an effective piece of propaganda? What would you have thought of it if you had been living in 1916 and had several relations in the armed forces?

6 Do *you* think people should be allowed to be conscientious objectors? Explain your answer.

7 How do *you* think conscientious objectors should be treated?

8 Look at your answers for questions 6 and 7. Would you have held the same opinion in 1916?

9 Do one of these pieces of writing as if you were living in 1916.

(a) Your son has just received his call-up. He announces he is a conscientious objector. Write a letter to him explaining your feelings.

(b) You have been fighting in the trenches for a year. Both your elder brothers have been killed. You are in hospital at the moment recovering from a bad wound and suffering from shell shock. You now doubt the whole point of the war and certainly criticise the way it is being conducted. You have just received two pieces of news. You are being awarded the Military Cross for bravery and your only remaining brother has been called up. Write a letter to him trying to persuade him not to join up.

10 Do you agree with Source G? Would you fight for your country? Under what circumstances? Prepare for a class debate on this topic.

ABYSSINIA: INTRODUCTION

In November 1930, Ras Tafari was crowned Emperor of Abyssinia, taking the name of Haile Selassie I. His full title was King of Kings, Lion of Judah, showing that Abyssinian rulers went back to biblical times, claiming descent from King Solomon. Abyssinia and Liberia were the only two countries in Africa not ruled by European states. Abyssinia had joined the League of Nations in 1924, and Haile Selassie began to introduce many new ideas into politics and society to bring his country up to date.

Abyssinia (now called Ethiopia) was a land of dry, hot, dusty soil and high central mountains. It relied on coffee as its main export crop, but it was hard to manage farming within the small scattered villages. Drought and hunger have always been features of life in this part of Africa. In spite of this, several European countries were interested in taking control of the country, but they found the local people determined to fight for their land.

In the 1880s, Italy became very concerned to occupy land in Africa, and moved into Eritrea, the northern province of Abyssinia. The British did not seem to mind these advances since Italy was less of a threat than France or other European nations. Italy also occupied Somaliland, to the east of Abyssinia (see the map below). However, the Abyssinian peoples united their forces at Adowa in 1896. The resulting battle was a crushing defeat for the Italians, who lost 6000 men. This was the only time that a native African army had managed to defeat a European army, and Italian troops were forced to withdraw from Abyssinia. The defeat was never forgotten in Italy.

Abyssinia, September 1935.

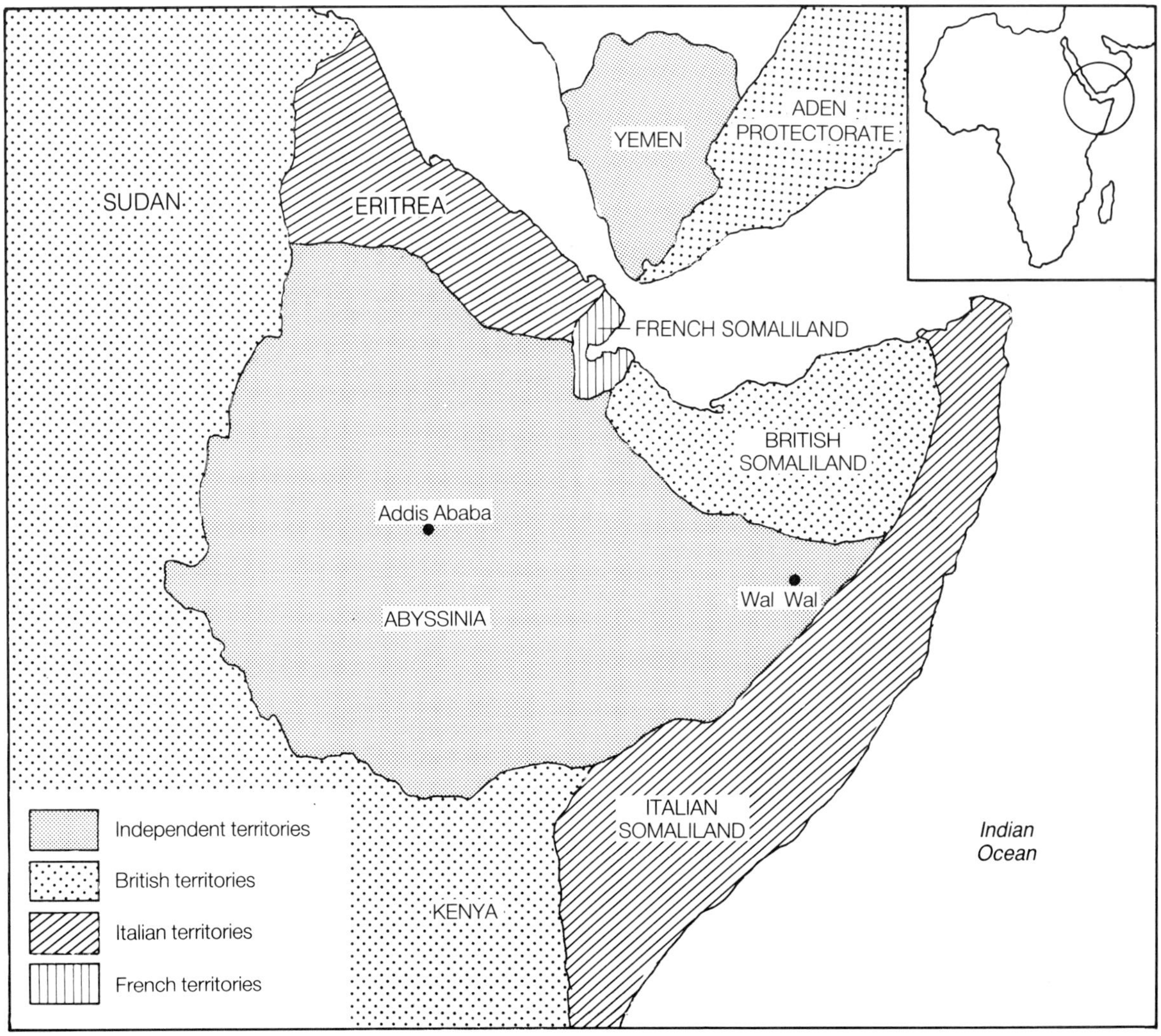

Legend:
- Independent territories
- British territories
- Italian territories
- French territories

In 1923, Benito Mussolini became leader (Il Duce) of Italy. His new Fascist party was determined to make Italy powerful and strong, so he concentrated on building up the armed forces. He also improved the economy and became a very important European leader. He made it clear that Italy wanted to expand its overseas Empire, even talking about creating a new Roman Empire. To such a leader, Adowa was a defeat that had to be avenged.

The Wal-Wal Incident 1934

600 men from the Abyssinian army were escorting British officials from Addis Ababa to inspect the frontiers. They stopped at the oasis of Wal-Wal for water and supplies. They found that a new fort had been built there by the Italian army. The Italian soldiers in the fort refused to talk; shots were fired and the Abyssinian commander was killed.

The Abyssinian mounted troops were easily defeated by Italian armoured cars and aircraft. Mussolini demanded an apology from Abyssinia. Emperor Haile Selassie decided to appeal to the League of Nations. After an emergency debate, the League decided to send investigators to decide who fired the first shot. The Italians issued an apology, but began to build up their troops in Italian Somaliland.

Less than a year later, in October 1935, the Abyssinians were back at the League, this time claiming the Italians had launched a full-scale invasion into Abyssinian territory.

The Emperor Haile Selassie with his bodyguard, 1935.

IS ITALY ATTACKING ABYSSINIA?

It is 5 October 1935. The problem facing the Assembly and Council of the League of Nations is as follows: the delegation from Abyssinia claim that their country has been invaded by Italy and they want something done about it.

There will be a meeting of the Assembly to discuss the issue, and after a vote has been taken, the Council will decide on a course of action.

The League of Nations

The main jobs of the League of Nations were as follows:

1 To prevent war.
2 To protect small or weak states.
3 To sort out border disputes and decide who owned what.
4 To run relief agencies for refugees and displaced persons.
5 To sort out international agreements and treaties.

Sir Samuel Hoare, the British Foreign Minister said in 1935:
'The League stands and my country stands with it . . . for the steady and collective resistance to acts of unprovoked aggression.'

In the *Assembly* issues were debated by all member states of the League of Nations. Delegates would stand up and make speeches; all member states had one vote each at the end of a debate. The Assembly also voted on the budget and admitted new members.

The resolution before the Assembly on this occasion is as follows. 'This assembly believes that the war in Abyssinia has been principally caused by Italy.'

The *Council* made sure that decisions made by the Assembly were carried out. It discussed the best way that the League could use its influence or power in a practical way. It consisted of five permanent members – Britain, France, Italy, Germany and Japan (in 1930) and up to ten temporary members elected for a term of one year.

The *Secretariat* prepared discussion papers and recorded debates of the Assembly and the Council. It also kept a record of the activities of all the League's agencies (such as the International Labour Organisation). It kept an eye on long-term problems such as health or armaments.

The Secretariat had prepared a paper outlining the evidence presented by Abyssinia for the forthcoming debate.

SOURCE A
Photographic evidence

An Abyssinian village after an Italian raid, 3 October 1935.

SOURCE B   Photographic evidence   *Attack on an Abyssinian village, 3 October 1935.*

The Evidence

Instructions

All these sources have been supplied as evidence by the Abyssinian delegation. You will need to consider them carefully when you take part in the debate on pages 14–15.

SOURCE C   Documentary evidence

Please to report arrival of goods STOP It is estimated they will be ready against xxxx by the end of the month STOP I am now awaiting orders before xxxx STOP (Unsigned)

Intercept of a telegram from Somalia to the Air Ministry in Rome. Experts have cast doubts upon its authenticity.

SOURCE D   Personal evidence

The Emperor of Abyssinia, Haile Selassie is in Geneva for the Assembly Debate. He reminds delegates that this is the second time that he has brought a complaint against Italy. The special investigators who have been appointed by the League to see whether Italian troops have any right to be at Wal-Wal have not yet reported back. It is clear, however, that Italy was in the wrong then, as she is now. Haile Selassie has hundreds of reports from the regions of Abyssinia which have been invaded, and he has sent his entire army to the region although he has not personally visited the battle zones. He feels that it is more important, as leader of his people, to get the backing of the world – he reminds all delegates: 'It is our turn to be attacked today. Tomorrow it may be yours.'

An eyewitness account.

ABYSSINIA: THE DEBATE AND THE DECISION

Part A: Assembly

Instructions

You are members of the League of Nations Assembly. Your teacher will split you up into six groups and give you your country's briefing from **Resource B**. You will represent five countries which take part in the debate (Abyssinia, Britain, France, Austria and Italy). The sixth group will act as the observers, who represent all the other members of the Assembly who do not speak in the debate.

Each of the five countries will be asked to speak for five minutes in the debate, after they have considered the evidence on pages 12 and 13 and prepared their case.

Delegates will be required to speak in the following order: first: Abyssinia; second: Austria; third: Britain; fourth: France; fifth: Italy. Each of these five countries will have one vote at the end of the debate.

The observer's group should note what is said during the debate, and will have two votes to cast at the end (representing the other countries in the League).

Your teacher will act as Chairman and will check that the following rules are observed:

1 No interruptions, shouting or heckling during speeches.
2 Points of order may be raised from the floor.
3 Speeches are limited to five minutes, in the order shown above.
4 Any of the above countries which fails to make a speech loses its right to vote.
5 Voting will be by a show of hands (one vote per country) at the end of the debate.

6 Those voting *for* the resolution will be saying that Italy is to blame for starting the war in Abyssinia; those voting *against* will be saying there is not sufficient evidence to prove that Italy has started a war.

The main points to be covered by the speeches might include the following.

(a) A statement of your country's view of international affairs.
(b) A consideration of the evidence – is it fair? Biased? Backed up by your own evidence? Real? What does it show?
(c) Your view of Italy and its leaders.
(d) Your view of the League of Nations.
(e) Your views on war and the rights of countries to take action.
(f) What the League might do in the future.

At the end of the debate, the Chairman will record the votes cast.

If there is a majority *for* the motion (that Italy is to blame), go on to Part B: Decision by the Council.

If there is a majority *against* the motion go straight on to the written exercises of the Teachers Resource Book.

NB There are seven votes (one per country plus two by the observer's group) to be cast.

Part B: Decision by the Council

If the Assembly decides that Italy has invaded Abyssinia, there are five possible options open to the Council.

1 Expel Italy from the League

This will mean that Italy will be outside the protection of the League, and will have fewer friends in the world. On withdrawing from Abyssinia, Italy will be re-admitted to membership. This is a very serious step, which has not been followed before. However, remember that many countries (including the USA, Germany and Japan) are not members of the League.

2 Send further investigators

The last investigators into the Wal-Wal Incident have still not reported even though they have

Haile Selassie addresses the League of Nations in 1936.

been hard at work for six months. It is difficult to establish good communications with Africa, but an investigation will confirm the evidence and help the Assembly. It may well be over a year before the report is ready, however.

3 Full economic sanctions

Many members of the League trade with Italy – for example, Britain exports coal, oil, clothing, and foodstuffs to Italy and imports luxury goods and foodstuffs from Italy. The Council could order all members to stop trading with Italy until it withdraws from Abyssinia and stops fighting.

To be quite clear about which goods and services would be prohibited, the Council has drawn up a list.

1 Coal.   4 Food.
2 Oil.   5 Loans.
3 War material. 6 No imports from Italy.

4 Partial sanctions

You need not include everything on your list of sanctions if you feel that the innocent may suffer as well as the guilty. It may be enough merely to remind Italy that it needs to trade. Therefore you may decide to ban only three out of the six possible areas listed above – e.g. coal, oil and food. Make clear which goods or services you are banning, and why.

5 Military action

This is the strongest possible response to an act of aggression. In this case, it would mean either sending naval or land forces to blockade Italy to prevent the movement of troops or goods, or sending an army or aircraft to Abyssinia to fight there. In either case, the action would have to be very swift and decisive – neither Britain nor France, the major military powers, have the aircraft or troops for a long campaign. This action would be very expensive and involve mobilisation of huge numbers. The League has no troops or aircraft of its own to send into action.

Instructions

After the debate in the Assembly, the Council decides on action. Each Council member – Britain, France, Italy and Austria (a temporary

member) – has one vote. The observers (who represent other Council members) have a casting vote in the event of a tie.

The Chairman will read through the options one at a time, after the delegates have returned from considering their strategy.

The option with the most votes (maximum four) will be the one that is carried.

After all the voting has been completed, your teacher will give you **Worksheet 2** to fill in.

British cartoon, 1935.

THE AWFUL WARNING.

FRANCE AND ENGLAND (together?).

"WE DON'T WANT YOU TO FIGHT,
BUT, BY JINGO, IF YOU DO,
WE SHALL PROBABLY ISSUE A JOINT MEMORANDUM
SUGGESTING A MILD DISAPPROVAL OF YOU."

ABYSSINIA: WHAT ACTUALLY HAPPENED

1 Clash between Italian and Abyssinian troops occurred at Wal-Wal in December 1934.

2 The incident was brought up at the League. The Italians apologised and agreed to look into the clash: but they did little, and started to build up troops in Italian Somaliland.

3 Britain and France met Italy at Stresa in April, 1935, and they knew that Italy was up to something. However, because they were worried about Mussolini going into alliance with Germany, they did not warn the Italians to leave Abyssinia alone.

4 Because of this, Mussolini thought he could attack Abyssinia and get away with it.

5 On 2 October, 1935, the invasion began.

6 However, public opinion in Britain and France dictated that their governments do something about it. At their instigation the Council took action, with only Austria, Hungary, and Albania supporting Italy. The measures taken were:

(a) prohibition of export of arms;
(b) prohibition of loans to Italy;
(c) prohibition of imports from Italy;
(d) prohibition of certain exports to Italy.

However they still supplied Italy with essentials such as steel, iron and coal, and the USA was not involved. The measures were largely cosmetic, designed to maintain the credibility of the League.

7 So, the Italian war effort was not really damaged. They carried on attacking Abyssinia.

8 Britain and France, however, started to worry about the Italian reaction to the economic sanctions which they had instigated. In December 1935, the British and French foreign ministers met in Paris to try and work out a deal by which Italy would get what it wanted with the minimum of trouble. This deal, known as the 'Hoare-Laval pact', would have given Italy two-thirds of Abyssinia.

9 Unfortunately for Italy, details of the deal leaked out. So great was the public opinion backlash that the French government lost power, and Eden, the British foreign secretary, was forced to take a much harder line. He was trying to get oil added to the list of embargoed goods when Germany invaded the Rhineland, directing attention away from Italy.

10 By May 1936, Italy had won, and its victory was recognised by the League in June when the sanctions were ended.

11 Britain and France had still succeeded in annoying Italy enough to force it into alliance with Germany.

SOURCE A
British cartoon.

THE MAN WHO TOOK THE LID OFF.

A modern historian, Anthony Wood, wrote this about the Abyssinian affair:

'The whole of the Abyssinian episode...meant nothing less than the utter bankruptcy of the League of Nations and the ideal of collective security. By antagonising Italy and yet failing to resist her, the two western powers had fallen hopelessly between two stools.'

SOURCE C

I, Haile Selassie, Emperor of Abyssinia, am here today to claim that justice which is due to my people and the assistance promised to it eight months ago when fifty nations asserted that aggression had been committed...I assert that the problem submitted to the Assembly today is a much wider one than the removal of sanctions...It is the very existence of the League of Nations...it is the value of promises made to small states that their integrity and independence be respected and endured. God and history will remember your judgements...Does this mean in practice the abandonment of Abyssinia to her aggressor? Representatives of the world, I have come to Geneva to discharge...the most painful duties of a Head of State. What reply shall I take back to my people...?

Haile Selassie speaking in the 1936 Debate as to whether partial sanctions against Italy should be lifted.

SOURCE D

The House may take it from me that, from the very moment this controversy started, we have left the Italian Government in no doubt whatever as to our attitude.

The criticism against the slowness of the League was not a fair one. What perhaps was surprising and encouraging was the way that the League has moved steadily forward during the last few weeks.

We do not believe that economic pressure of the kind envisaged would be ineffective, and we believe, on the other hand, that if it was collectively applied it would definitely shorten the duration of the war.

The French interpret Article 16 of the Covenant as we interpret it. In the event of an isolated attack, inconceivable though such madness might be, we and they and the rest of the League stand together and resist it with our full and united force. Further, from the beginning of the present deliberations at Geneva until now there has been no discussion of military sanctions and no such measures therefore have formed any part of our policy.

The League must stand together and it must walk together. The League is a great instrument of peace. Let the critics remember that fact when they say we ought to close the Suez Canal at once...Do they mean that we should do it alone? If so, what becomes of collective security and the argument that this is not a quarrel between Great Britain and Italy?

Sir Samuel Hoare speaking to the House of Commons, 23 October 1935.

SOURCE B

British cartoon.

GUERNICA: INTRODUCTION

Nationalist troops during the Spanish Civil War.

SOURCE A *Spain, 1937.*

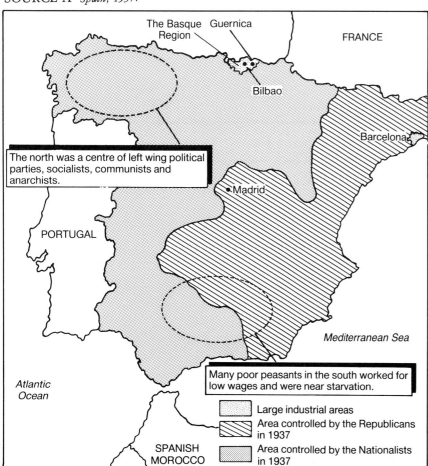

The north was a centre of left wing political parties, socialists, communists and anarchists.

Many poor peasants in the south worked for low wages and were near starvation.

- Large industrial areas
- Area controlled by the Republicans in 1937
- Area controlled by the Nationalists in 1937

Background to the Spanish Civil War 1936–39

Before 1931, Spain was ruled by a king supported by the rich, the Catholic Church, the police (Civil Guard) and the army.

But Spain had many problems. The large industrial areas were in decline. The workers suffered from unemployment and poverty. In the south, most of the people were peasants who worked for very low wages, close to starvation, on the estates of rich landowners.

This created a large group of discontented Spaniards. The north, in particular, was a hotbed of political groups: socialists, communists and even anarchists who opposed the king.

In 1931, King Alfonso XIII abdicated and Spain became a republic. Reform came too slowly to please the poor and there was much civil disorder. As a result, the army, led by General Francisco Franco tried to seize control. Franco and his Fascists were given money and troops by other European dictators, notably Hitler and Mussolini.

Franco's forces, known as the Nationalists, were opposed by the Republicans. The Republicans were supported by foreign volunteers who formed the *International Brigade*, and by some money and arms from Russia.

During the civil war, which lasted for three years, about half a million people died. In March 1939, General Franco and his Nationalist forces were victorious.

League of Nations Investigation

In April 1937, an incident took place in Guernica, a town in the Basque region of northern Spain.

Instructions

You are members of a League of Nations investigation team whose task is to discover what happened. Work carefully through Sources A–I on pages 18–21 filling in **Worksheet 3** which your teacher will give you. When you have finished, answer the questions on pages 19–21.

SOURCE B

DESTRUCTION OF GUERNICA
Priest's Account
"SKY BLACK WITH PLANES"

A message has been received by the London delegate of the Basque Government stating that Father Alberto Onaindia, Dean of the Cathedral at Valladolid, is on his way to lay before the Pope a statement on the recent aerial bombardment of Guernica. The following details of his report were received in London yesterday:—

"I was in Bilbao when the Basque Government decided to evacuate Guernica, where I had friends and relations. I arrived at Guernica on April 26 at 4.40 p.m. I had hardly left the car when the bombardment began. The people were terrified. They fled, abandoning their live stock in the marketplace. The bombardment lasted until 7.45 p.m. During that time five minutes did not elapse without the sky being black with German aeroplanes."

METHOD OF ATTACK

"The method of attack was always the same. First there was machine-gun fire, then ordinary bombs, and finally incendiary. The planes descended very low, the machine-gun fire tearing up the woods and roads, in whose gutters, huddled together, lay old men, women, and children. Before long it was impossible to see as far as 500 metres owing to the heavy smoke occasioned by the bombardment."

Fire enveloped the whole city. Screams of lamentation were heard everywhere and the people, filled with terror, knelt, lifting their hands to heaven as if to implore divine protection.

"The 'planes descended to 200 metres, letting loose a terrible machine-gun fire. I reached my car and just had time to take refuge in a small group of oaks. I have not heard of any inhabitants who survived among the ill and wounded in the hospitals."

"The first hours of the night presented a terrible spectacle of men and women in the woods outside the city searching for their families and friends. Most of the corpses were riddled with bullets."

Extract from the Manchester Guardian, *3 May 1937.*

SOURCE C

A German experiment?
THE TRAGEDY OF GUERNICA
TOWN DESTROYED IN AIR ATTACK

EYE-WITNESS'S ACCOUNT
From Our Special Correspondent
BILBAO, APRIL 27

CHURCH BELL ALARM

In the form of its execution and the scale of the destruction it wrought, no less than in the selection of its objective, the raid on Guernica is unparalleled in military history. Guernica was not a military objective. A factory producing war material lay outside the town and was untouched. So were two barracks some distance from the town. The town lay far behind the lines. The object of the bombardment was seemingly the demoralization of the civil population and the destruction of the cradle of the Basque race.

The tactics of the bombers, which may be of interest to students of the new military science, were as follows: — First, small parties of aeroplanes threw heavy bombs and hand grenades all over the town, choosing area after area in orderly fashion. Next came fighting machines which swooped low to machine-gun those who ran in panic from dugouts, some of which had already been penetrated by 1,000 lb. bombs, which make a hole 25 ft. deep. Many of these people were killed as they ran. A large herd of sheep being brought in to the market was also wiped wiped out. The object of this move was apparently to drive the population under-ground again, for next as many as 12 bombers appeared at a time dropping heavy and incendiary bombs upon the ruins. The rhythm of this bombing of an open town was, therefore, a logical one: first, hand grenades and heavy bombs to stampede the population, then machine-gunning to drive them below, next heavy and incendiary bombs to wreck the houses and burn them on top of their victims.

Extract from The Times, *28 April 1937.*

SOURCE D

Cartoon of Franco and Hitler by Allorza
from La Vanguardia *(1937).*

Questions

Look at Sources A–E.

1 Why might Guernica be a target for the Nationalists?

2 What are the main differences between the story told in Source B and that told in Source C?

3 What was the relationship between Hitler and General Franco according to Source D?

4 How do you think the house in Source E was damaged? Why do you think this?

SOURCE E
Guernica, April 1937.

WHAT HAPPENED AT GUERNICA?

Questions

Look at Sources F–I.

1 How did Cardozo say Guernica was destroyed? (Source F).

2 Pick three words or phrases which show what Lord Lothian thought of Hitler. (Source G)

3 In what way does source H support or contradict the evidence given in Source F?

4 How is the story told in Source I similar to the story told in Source B? How is it different?

Using all the sources.

5 Use the League of Nations Investigation Sheets to prepare a report for the League. In this you should explain:
(a) what happened at Guernica;
(b) how it happened;
(c) who caused it;
(d) your reasons for thinking this.

6 The sources do not all agree.
(a) Summarise the two different stories they tell.
(b) Explain why they tell two different stories.
(c) Which story do you believe? Explain why you think this.

7 In 1936, Britain signed an agreement with France that no foreign country should interfere in the Spanish Civil War. What was the likely reaction in Britain to the newspaper reports in Sources B and H?

SOURCE F

The Republicans were countering the Nationalist offensive against Bilbao with a propaganda offensive of their own; at this time it was concentrated on the famous Guernica incident . . . The story circulated – and widely believed – was that Guernica, an open town, was destroyed by incendiary bombs dropped by Nationalist aircraft; Cardozo was indignant at the success it was having in England. He was in Guernica immediately after its occupation by the Nationalists, and so was able to make a pretty thorough examination. It was clear to him, he said, that the Republicans themselves had set fire to the town before leaving . . . Certainly Guernica was bombed by the Nationalists, but it was not an open town at the time it was bombed; it was packed with Republican troops, and was, in fact, a divisional headquarters.

Extract from Mine Were of Trouble *by P. Kemp (1957).*

SOURCE G

The British people yearned for good relations with Germany. When the situation had so greatly improved . . . some mischance, such as press reports (on Guernica) gave certain evil forces an opportunity to check progress, but the growing strength of British opinion regarding friendly relations with Germany was such that he felt he wished to confirm if possible the convinced beliefs of the Chancellor regarding our future relationship.

Lord Lothian talking to Hitler on 4 May 1937.

SOURCE H

REBELS INVITE JOURNALISTS TO THEIR AERODROMES
Anxiety to Escape Responsibility

ST. JEAN DE LUZ, APRIL, 28.

Salamanca at two o'clock this morning formally and officially denied all knowledge of the raid on Guernica. General Franco's headquarters say that no 'plane left the Vitoria aerodrome after Monday afternoon and there was no flying at all on Tuesday, April 27. Foreign journalists at Vitoria and San Sebastian, have been invited, it is stated, to visit the aerodrome and verify these facts by inspection of the essential records, pilot's log-books, petrol registers, etc.

The routine Salamanca communique issued at 6 p.m. yesterday and released at midnight mentions that there were no air activities on the Biscay front the day before on account of poor weather.

The insurgent authorities do not deny that the raid of Guernica occurred, but they declare in the most positive way that they had no part in it. Whether this is mere propaganda or whether it conceals some deep mystery it is as yet impossible to say. This bombardment is of very great importance in view of the religious and mystic veneration which every Basque throughout the world has for Guernica, the holy city of the Basques.

BASQUE MANIFESTO

In a new proclamation vigorously denying rebel suggestions that Guernica and Eibar had been destroyed by the Republicans themselves, Señor Aguirre, the Basque President, to-day declared:

Before God and before the posterity that will judge us all I affirm that for the space of three and a half hours German aeroplanes bombarded the defenceless civil population of the historic city of Guernica with unexampled savagery. They reduced it to ashes, pursuing with machine-gun fire women and children, who perished in great numbers, while the remainder fled insane with terror.

I ask the civilised world if it can countenance the extermination of a people which has always guarded as its most precious principle the defence of its liberty and of its civil democracy, which the thousand-year-old tree of Guernica has symbolised for centuries.

I want to believe that the nations will respond with assistance for the more than 300,000 women and children who are coming to take refuge in Bilbao. We ask nothing for the men, since our firm resolve to defend the liberty of our people will cause us to face the greatest sacrifices with a calm spirit and a tranquil conscience.

REBELS' SUPERIORITY IN 'PLANES

"The German and Italian General Staff at Deva is directing the most brutal onslaught of the civil war," states a communiqué published by the representatives of the Basque Government. "The insurgents have a hundred aeroplanes on the Basque front, whereas the Basque Government has practical use of none."

"The Basque troops maintain admirable moral while awaiting help, which has not yet arrived."—Reuter.

Extract from the Manchester Guardian, *29 April 1937.*

SOURCE I

She visited the remains of Guernica in the company of another Nationalist press officer, Ignacio Rosalles. 'We arrived in Guernica to find it a lonely chaos of timber and brick, like an ancient civilization in process of being excavated. There were only three or four people in the streets. An old man was clearing away debris. Accompanied by Rosalles, my official escort, I went up to him and asked if he had been in the town during the destruction. He nodded his head and, when I asked what had happened, waved his arms in the air and declared that the sky had been black with planes – "*Aviones*," he said: "*Italianos y alemanes.*" Rosalles was astonished. "Guernica was burned," he contradicted heatedly. The old man, however, stuck to his point, insisting that after a four-hour bombardment there was little left to burn. Rosalles moved me away. "He's a red", he explained indignantly. A couple of days later, we were talking to some staff officers. Rosalles described our drive along the coast and told them of the incident at Guernica. "The town was full of reds," he said. "They tried to tell us it was bombed, not burnt." The tall staff officer replied: "But of course it was bombed. We bombed it and bombed it and bombed it, and *bueno*, why not?" Rosalles looked astonished, and when we were back in the car again he said, "I don't think I would write about that if I were you." '

An eyewitness account, from The Spanish Civil War *by P. Preston (1983).*

Exercises

8 Write a newspaper article to follow one of these headlines in 1937.
(a) The lesson of Guernica. Are we next?
(b) Don't knock Adolf! We need all the friends we can get.

9 Research what the League actually did about the Spanish Civil War and suggest reasons why it followed this policy.

10 You have now done two League of Nations investigations, the first: 'Is Italy invading Abyssinia?' and the second: 'What happened at Guernica?'. Compare these two investigations. You should cover the following points:
(a) the quality of the evidence;
(b) the reliability of the evidence;
(c) how easy/difficult it was to reach a conclusion and why.

11 On the basis of these investigations and any other research you have done, write a short essay about the League of Nations. You should cover the following points:
(a) weaknesses of the League;
(b) how useful the League was as an organisation for settling international disputes;
(c) a notable failure of the League.

THE PROBLEM

SOURCE A

Date	Harvest (millions of tons)	Average yield (centner per hectare)
1913	80	–
1921	42	5.5
1924	51.4	6.2
1925	72.5	8.3

Grain harvests in Russia.

SOURCE B

The civil war in Russia affected farming regions very badly, with land being ruined and crops being destroyed. It is estimated that five million people died during the famine.

Two doctors working in the Ufa region, reported that people were so desperate for food that they would do anything. They claimed the following story was typical:

'A Tartar killed a 13 year old girl, a relative, who had come to visit him, by hitting her over the head with a log. He not only ate her but also cut off from her several pounds of fat, which he sold at the market.'

The famine of 1921–2. L. and L. Vasilievski, Kniga o golode (1922).

SOURCE C   *A peasant farmer in the mid 1920s.*

SOURCE D   *Threshing grain in Russia, 1920.*

SOURCE E

The symbol of the unproductive peasant was the wooden plough which was still the peasants' main tool. As late as 1928, 5.5 million peasant holdings were still using this ancient implement which was at least as old as the Pharaohs... Three-quarters of the land was sown by hand; 40% of the harvest was threshed with the flail, and almost half of it reaped with the sickle and the scythe.

The farms were often too small for it to be profitable to keep a horse... it was not unusual to see a wretched old wooden plough... dragged along... by the farmer, or even his wife.

There was an aspect of the situation which was even worse. The lands belonging to one peasant were not grouped together but widely scattered in single strips.

A modern historian.

SOURCE F

It was absolutely necessary for Russia, if we were to avoid periodic famine, to plough the land with tractors. We must mechanize our agriculture. When we gave tractors to the peasants they were spoiled in a few months. Only collective farms with workshops could handle tractors. We took the greatest trouble to explain it to the peasants. It was no use arguing with them. After you have said all you can to a peasant he says he must go home and consult his wife, and he must consult his herder...

Stalin speaking to Churchill, from W. S. Churchill, The Second World War *(1951) Vol. IV.*

Questions

1(a) What does Source A say was wrong with agriculture in the USSR?

(b) Why would the Bolsheviks (the new government) be unlikely to publish these figures?

2(a) What was the major problem in Russia in 1922 according to Source B?

(b) Give reasons why Source B might be unreliable.

3(a) What do Sources C and D tell you about Soviet agriculture?

(b) Do they tell the whole story? Explain your answer.

(c) Describe the methods of agriculture being used in these pictures. What is wrong with them?

(d) Do these photographs support or contradict the evidence given in Source E?

(e) List three problems faced by the farmer shown in Source C in 1923?

4(a) What was the general state of Soviet agriculture according to Source E?

(b) What evidence does the writer of Source E give to back up his conclusions about agriculture?

(c) Is Source E a primary or secondary source? Was its information available to (i) Stalin; (ii) Soviet farmers in 1925?

5(a) What does Stalin (Source F) say is wrong with Soviet agriculture?

(b) What did (i) Stalin; and (ii) Soviet farmers think about tractors being used on the land?

(c) What clues does Source F give you as to the *way* that Stalin operated? Was he firm or soft, clear or muddled, tolerant or intolerant?

THE SOLUTION

Questions

1 Explain carefully how a collective farm works using the evidence on these pages.

2 What did collective farms get from the towns? What did they give to the towns?

3 What was the main advantage that collective farms gave to Stalin's general policy?

4 Select one of the following methods to explain collectivisation to the peasants of the Ukraine in 1929.

(a) A poster to be displayed in every village.

(b) A personal letter from Stalin to be sent to every household.

(c) A speech to be given to the peasants by the local Communist party official.

5 Explain the choice you made for question 4, then design, draw or write the poster, letter or speech.

One possible solution to the problems of Soviet agriculture was the development of the collective farm (kolkhoz). A kolkhoz was a very large farm, formed by peasants pooling their land and animals, which then became the property of the collective. The members of the kolkhoz were paid wages for the work they did but any profits went to the kolkhoz to buy new machines, livestock or crops. Machines such as tractors or combine harvesters could be supplied by the new factories built under the First Five Year Plan (1927–32).

A typical kolkhoz, 1937.

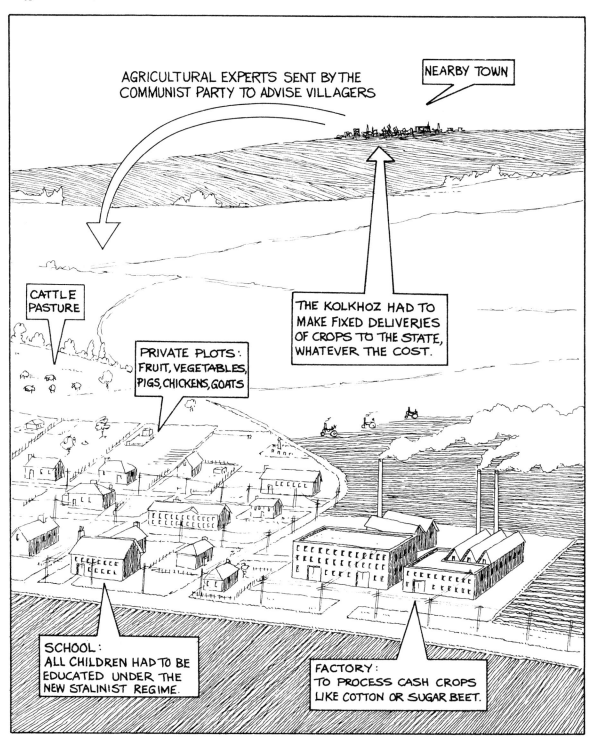

24

SOURCE A

What is the way out? The way out is to turn the small and scattered peasant farms into large united farms gradually but surely, not by pressure, but by example and persuasion, into large farms based on common, co-operative, collective cultivation of the land . . . There is no other way out.

Joseph Stalin, 1927.

In 1928, about 3% of the total land being farmed in the USSR was organised into collective farms. The First Five Year Plan calculated that up to 20% of output would come from collective farms by 1933. However, the pace of change was set by Stalin at breakneck speed so that there could be no growth of opposition to his plans. In March 1930, Stalin announced that 58% of land in Russia had been collectivised. Stalin blamed 'over-zealous officials' for the speed of change.

A visitor to the USSR, Maurice Hindus, went to see his friend, Yekim Lavrentin, a peasant farmer in 1929. The peasants from Yekim's village explained how they felt about collectivisation.

Questions

6 What was the general reaction of the villagers pictured below to the idea of collectivisation?

7 What would these villagers do if it was suggested that they should join a collective or state farm?

8 The comments below were made during a village meeting. Write two reports on this meeting:
(a) as the leader of the village;
(b) as a Communist official, reporting to OGPU (the secret police).
Describe their feelings and ideas in each case.

THE OUTCOME

The three peasants described below are typical of
the millions of people who farmed land in central
and southern USSR in the 1920s.

The blacksmith

Lukyan owns two acres of land in the village,
along with his blacksmith's forge. He spends
most of his time working on his land, helping
other villagers and mending tools. He grows
wheat on some of his land and some he allows
others to use for free grazing. He also makes
horseshoes which he trades for eggs or vegetables.

He believes strongly in tradition and old
methods. He refuses to make an iron ploughshare
as he believes it will be unlucky.

Lukyan has no animals of his own, but he has
an excellent supply of food through trading his
skills. He often makes a meal for friends and occa-
sionally throws a party for the whole village. He
is, therefore, respected by the villagers and something of a leader.

His two sons were killed fighting for the Red
Army against the Whites in 1920.

The bedniak (poor peasant)

Eva owns one acre of land in the village, as well as
a few pigs, geese and one very old, thin cow. Her
husband was killed in an accident two years ago,
leaving her to raise six children.

Eva cannot sell her land or move away from the
village, so she works the land herself. She has to
borrow a plough from her neighbours. Her two
eldest children put the yoke of the plough over
their necks and pull it along. She sows seed by
hand, digs the soil with a wooden shovel, and cuts
wheat with a bill-hook.

Her land has always grown wheat, which she
gives the state as payment for her taxes. She works
14 hours a day, seven days a week on her own
land. She cannot read or write.

The kulak (rich peasant)

Sergei owns ten acres of land in the village, dotted about in various strips. His wife died some years ago, but he has one son, Nikolai, whom he hires out as a shepherd or general labourer during the summer.

Sergei works his own land as well as land on the local State Farm (sovkhoz). Last year he saved all his wages from the sovkhoz and bought a spinning wheel and weaving frame. In winter he makes clothes which he sells at the local market. He has already made enough money to buy two cows and a horse.

He lives in a small hut, which was built by his grandfather, on the edge of the village. He grows wheat and barley in rotation, as well as peas and sugar beet.

Collectivisation report: instructions

You have been asked by the Central Committee to report on this village and in particular on these three households. Your report should cover the following points:

1 Who is the richest person?
2 Who works the hardest?
3 Who will have the most to lose if the village is collectivised?
4 Who will have the most to gain?
5 Will any of them support collectivisation?
6 How will a kolkhoz improve the village?
7 How might the villagers be persuaded to join a collective?
8 Who will be the most dangerous opponent of your plans?
9 What skills do they each have?
10 What do they own?

11 Who will be the most useful to the collective?

Note: The organisation of the report is left up to you. You need not cover all the points above, or you may wish to add more points of your own.

Destruction of the kulaks

It soon became clear that force would be necessary to persuade villagers to join collectives. In 1930, the Communist Party declared war on all kulaks.

'We must smash the kulaks. We must strike at the kulaks so hard as to prevent them rising to their feet again. We must wipe them out as a social class.'

All kulaks lost their property and possessions which were confiscated and added to the local kolkhoz. Kulak families were deported to new regions, either to farm in the icy north or to join work gangs in the industrial districts. The army was sent into villages to enforce these new rules and given orders to shoot anyone who resisted.

Deportation of the kulaks

Over two and a half million kulaks were deported between 1930 and 1932. Here are two eyewitness accounts.

SOURCE A

Trainloads of deported peasants left for the icy north, the forests, the steppes, the deserts. There were whole populations denuded of everything. The old folk starved to death in mid-journey, new born babies were buried on the banks of the roadside and each wilderness had its crop of little crosses.

SOURCE B

Stock was slaughtered every night. Hardly had dusk fallen when the muffled short bleats of sheep, the death squeals of pigs, or the lowing of calves could be heard. Both those who had joined the kolkhoz and individual farmers killed their stock. The dogs began to drag entrails about the village; cellars and barns were filled with meat. 'Kill, it's not ours any more. Kill, they'll take it for meat anyway.' They ate till they could eat no more. Young and old suffered from stomach ache.

Questions

1 What effects would this new policy have on Lukyan, Eva, Sergei and their families?

2 How would 'war on the kulaks' help Soviet agriculture?

3 Why did the peasants kill their own animals in 1930?

4 What evidence was there in your report that peasants might react this way?

5 How does the reality of collectivisation compare with Stalin's view of it?

6 Why was collectivisation slowed down after 1930?

DID IT WORK?

The questions for this section are on **Worksheet 4** which your teacher will give to you.

Yes

SOURCE A

Tell me, you wretched people, what hope is there for you if you remain on individual pieces of land... From year to year as you increase in population you divide and subdivide your strips of land. You cannot use machinery on your land because no machine man ever made could stand the rough ridges that the strip system creates. You will have to work in your own old ways and stew in your old misery. Don't you see that under your present system there is nothing ahead of you but ruin and starvation?

You accuse us of making false promises. Let us see. And please do not interrupt and do not giggle. Last year you got a schoolhouse, and have you forgotten how we of the Party and of the Soviet had to squeeze out of you, through voluntary tax, your share of the cost of the schoolhouse. And now? Aren't you glad that your children can attend school? Were we wrong when we urged you to build a fire station? Were we wrong when we urged you to lay decent bridges across your stream in the swamp? Were we wrong when we threatened to fine you if you didn't take home two loads of peat to mix with the bedding for your stock so as to have good fertiliser for your fields.

A Communist Party official speaks to the villagers about the kolkhoz, in Red Bread *by M. Hindus (1934).*

SOURCE B

Transporting grain from the Burevestnik collective farm, Stalingrad District. The banner refers to promises about grain deliveries.

SOURCE C

Stalin, ignoring the great cost in human life and misery, claimed that collectivisation was a success; for, after the great famines attending the amalgamation of the peasant farms were past, no more famines came to haunt the Russian people. The collective farms, despite all their inefficiencies, did grow more food than the tiny, privately-owned holdings had done; for example, 30–40 million tons of grain were produced every year. Collectivisation also meant the introduction of mechanisation into the countryside... Now two million hitherto backward peasants learned to drive a tractor. New methods of farming were taught by 110,000 engineering and agricultural experts. The countryside was indeed transformed.

E. Roberts, Stalin: Man of Steel *(1968).*

SOURCE D

A collective farm.

No

SOURCE E

	1928	1929	1930	1931	1932	1933
Grain harvest (million tons)	73.3	71.7	83.5	69.5	69.6	63.4
State grain procurements (million tons)	10.8	16.1	22.1	22.8	17.5	22.6
Livestock (million head)						
Cattle	70.5	67.1	52.5	47.9	40.7	38.4
Pigs	26.0	20.4	13.6	14.4	11.6	12.1
Sheep and goats	146.7	147.0	108.8	77.7	52.1	50.2

Collective farm production figures.

SOURCE F

There was mass starvation in the USSR in the winters of 1932 and 1933, on a far larger scale than the famine of 1920–21. It is estimated that 10–15 million people died of hunger during these years. Bread rationing was introduced into every town and city.

A modern historian.

SOURCE G

Starving children, 1931.

SOURCE H

Red Army soldiers planting a tree.

SOURCE I

Within a short time rural Russia became pandemonium. The overwhelming majority of the peasantry confronted the Government with desperate opposition. Collectivisation degenerated into a military operation, a cruel civil war. Rebellious villagers were surrounded by machine-guns and forced to surrender. Masses of Kulaks were deported to remote unpopulated lands in Siberia . . . The bulk of the peasants decided to bring in as little as possible of their property to the collective farms, which they imagined to be state owned factories, in which they themselves would become mere factory hands. In desperation they slaughtered their cattle, smashed implements and burned crops . . . Vast tracts of land were left untilled. Famine stalked the towns and black soil steppe of the Ukraine.

Isaac Deutscher, Stalin *(1949).*

CHARACTERS

Instructions on how to use the characters

In this section, you will find outlined six fictional characters. They represent a cross-section of people living in Germany during the years 1919–34. Although they have been made up, they could well have existed, and they have been made as realistic as possible. You and your teachers may decide to use these characters in one or more of the following ways:

1 Throughout the rest of this unit, there are questions and exercises designed to be answered by each of these characters. You should take on one character now, and use that person for all the remaining role-playing exercises. Later, your answers (and even life!) may depend on decisions you have made earlier, so think carefully each time. (Your answers could be recorded in the form of a dated diary, so that you can keep a record of how your character gets on throughout the years 1919–34).

2 Alternatively, you may answer the role-playing exercises from the point of view of several of the characters, so that you can see the attitudes and reactions of different kinds of people to Hitler's rise to power.

3 You could use the characters for role-playing discussions or dramatic situations. If you do so, you should give them suitable names, use costumes, props etc. to try to give as realistic a view of the characters as possible.

Character 1
Part A

You are a Civil Servant. You work in the Employment Office. Every day you talk to dozens of workers who have no jobs. All they do is complain and insult you as if it is your fault. You are reasonably well paid and extremely thankful that you are not unemployed like thousands of others.

You did not fight the war because your eyesight was bad. Your children were too young to be involved. The war seemed wasteful and pointless to you.

Part B

You often wonder if the fault for the unemployment lies with the workers who seem to be lazy, lacking purpose and too dissatisfied with life. A more hard-working attitude from them might make a big difference.

You would like to see old grievances about the Treaty of Versailles forgotten and for people to be more grateful for what they have. People should stop complaining and be happier, then they could get on with the job of putting Germany back on her feet.

Character 2
Parts A and B

You lost your husband in the war. Your son has been missing since 1916. Both were fighting on the Eastern Front. You managed to get a job in a grocer's shop and have worked very hard for some years. You are hoping to marry the owner. He is older than you, but he is kind and will look after you. This marriage will end all your troubles.

You feel sorry for the many poor people who come into the shop begging for food and you feel that something should be done to help them. However, you remember the terrible days of the war only too well and you feel that the only hope for the country is for the Germans to live at peace with their European neighbours. You think that peace will only come from co-operation.

You also believe that the most important qualities that a government should have are fairness and a voice for all. Dictatorships and empires, you believe, can only lead, in the long run, to more wars. You want to forgive and forget, and to let the government get on with its job.

Character 3
Part A

You are a nurse in a hospital for wounded and disabled servicemen. You see men with terrible handicaps all caused by the war. It seems such a waste to you that these men were injured and for nothing. The government seems to provide very little for these men – there is hardly any provision for them to have a decent pension in their old age.

Part B

You yourself are not very well paid and recently you have fallen into debt. You borrowed some money from a money lender who is now asking for payment. You are at your wits' end to know how to pay him. This is particularly worrying because you have a very clever 12-year-old child and you are trying to save up enough money to send her to a special school for clever children.

Character 4
Parts A and B

You are a rich industrialist. You invested money wisely in 1870 and you have made an enormous fortune from your industrial empire. Your factories produce iron and steel as well as camera lenses and electrical parts. Now many of your factories lie idle because of the slump in world trade. You feel very bitter about the lack of action by the government to help you.

Before and during the war you did especially well because of the arms deal you made with the German army. You supplied armour plate, photographic equipment, shell fuses and radio parts. You would obviously like to see these opportunities open to you again.

You would now like to forget the bad times and look forward to a more dynamic and powerful leadership which will get Germany out of its present mess and be prepared to build up armaments again.

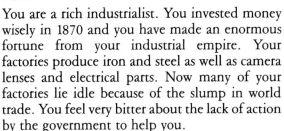

Character 5
Part A

You own a clothes shop in East Prussia. You lost your only son in the war. You are now expecting another baby. You are thrilled about this. Your main hope is that there will not be another war in which your child will have to fight and perhaps be killed.

Part B

Every time you go to visit your father in Germany you have to go through the Polish Corridor. The Polish border guards lock the German passengers into their carriages and lock shutters over the windows. They are often rude and insulting.

You survive the great inflation fairly well and although you do not completely approve of the present government you do not want a more aggressive government which might start another war.

Character 6
Part A

You are a mechanic. You have been out of work for four years and your family has suffered horribly from poverty.

You thought the war of 1914 was ridiculous. It certainly did nothing to help you and brought you nothing but hardship. You always believed it was absurd to fight for the glory of the Kaiser who was, in any case, pretty well off and always seemed to have enough to feed *his* family!

In 1918 you gladly joined the Spartacist Revolution which tried to stop the war. You did this because of the effects of the British blockade of Germany which was causing widespread starvation and shortages. What was the point of carrying on the war in the face of that?

Part B

You went to jail for two years. Since then you have been working for a fairer Germany where the wealthy will be made to share out their money. Most of the rich got their money from illegal activities in the war like keeping prices artificially high, overworking their employees and from supplying weapons which destroyed the poor workers of all the countries of Europe.

You hate war and poverty. You would like to see all the people of Europe united and working towards a fairer world.

THE WEIMAR REPUBLIC: INTRODUCTION

The Versailles settlement

SOURCE A

Europe after the Treaty of Versailles, 1919.

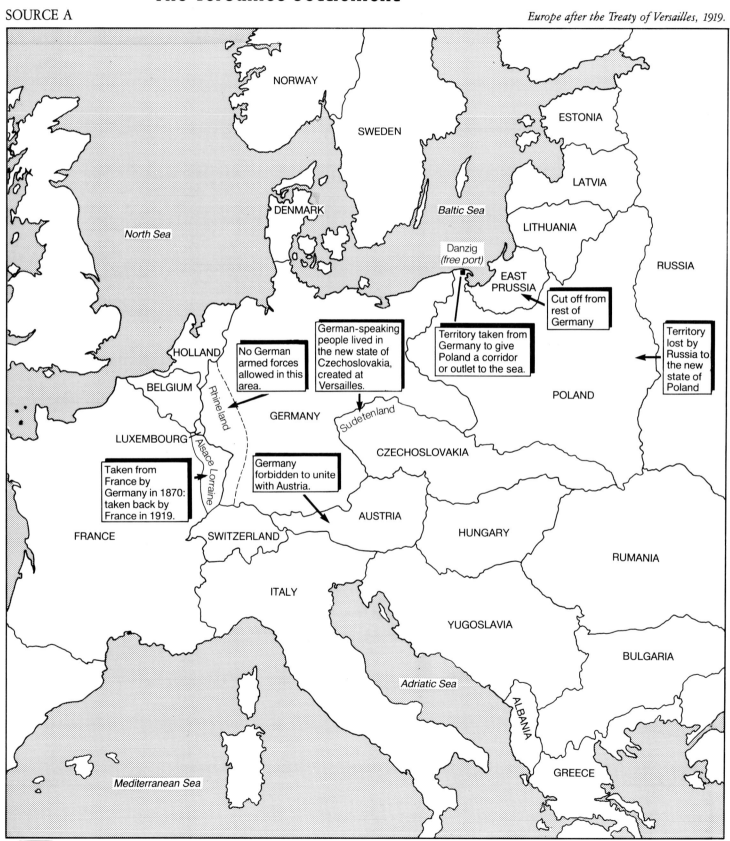

NORWAY

SWEDEN

ESTONIA

LATVIA

DENMARK

Baltic Sea

LITHUANIA

North Sea

RUSSIA

Danzig (free port)

EAST PRUSSIA

Cut off from rest of Germany

HOLLAND

Territory taken from Germany to give Poland a corridor or outlet to the sea.

Territory lost by Russia to the new state of Poland

German-speaking people lived in the new state of Czechoslovakia, created at Versailles.

No German armed forces allowed in this area.

BELGIUM

Rhineland

GERMANY

Sudetenland

POLAND

LUXEMBOURG

Alsace Lorraine

Germany forbidden to unite with Austria.

CZECHOSLOVAKIA

Taken from France by Germany in 1870: taken back by France in 1919.

FRANCE

SWITZERLAND

AUSTRIA

HUNGARY

RUMANIA

ITALY

YUGOSLAVIA

BULGARIA

Adriatic Sea

ALBANIA

GREECE

Mediterranean Sea

The Kaiser abdicated on 9 November 1918 and on 11 November, World War 1 ended. In January 1919 elections were held. The government met at Weimar in February to draw up the new constitution. However, the government faced problems right from the start.

Problems of the Weimar Government

1 There were terrible food shortages as a result of the British naval blockade against Germany during World War 1.

2 The Spartacist revolt, January 1919: communists, led by Karl Liebnecht and Rosa Luxemburg, seized important buildings in Berlin. The 'Freikorps' (volunteer ex-soldiers) put the revolt down and murdered the leaders.

3 The Kapp Revolt, January 1920: the Freikorps tried to seize Berlin but this was defeated when the workers went on a general strike.

SOURCE B

Vengeance! German Nation

Today in the Hall of Mirrors, the disgraceful Treaty is being signed. Do not forget it. The German people will with unceasing labour press forward to reconquer the place among nations to which it is entitled. Then will come vengeance for the shame of 1919.

A translation of the front page of Deutsche Zeitung, *28 June 1919.*

Questions

Look at Source A.

1 Why were no German armed forces allowed in the Rhineland?

2 Why was the Polish Corridor created?

3 What arrangements were made about Danzig?

4 Describe three other measures taken against Germany in the Treaty which did *not* concern territorial changes.

5 How did the arrangements made for Austria and the Sudetenland break the Principle of National Self-determination laid down by the Treaty of Versailles?

Look at Source B.

6 What did many Germans think about the Treaty? Why did they think this?

Look at Source C.

7 What does the cartoonist think about the Treaty?

8 Do you agree with his opinion? Explain your answer.

Your character

Look at the brief for your character. If it has two parts, read Part A only. Think about how he/she feels about the events of 1919–22.

9 Fill in **Worksheet 6**, which your teacher will give you, on behalf of your character.

10 Hold a class discussion and listen to the views of other people about the Versailles settlement.

11 Write a paragraph saying what you think the Germans felt about the Treaty in 1922.

SOURCE C

" PERHAPS IT WOULD GEE-UP BETTER IF WE LET IT TOUCH EARTH "

British cartoon.

CONSTITUTIONAL PROBLEMS

Questions

Look at Source A.

1 What system of voting was used?

2 What powers does the President have?

3 Which clause indicates that the Chancellor should have a majority in the Reichstag?

4 How might Clauses 115, 117, 118, 123 and 124 help an unscrupulous party and so threaten the safety of the Republic?

5 Why did the people who wrote the Weimar Constitution decide to use the proportional representation (PR) system of voting?

The Constitution

The Constitution of the Weimar Republic was designed to be a model of fairness and democracy. It aimed to create a state which was quite different from the autocratic empire of the Kaiser.

SOURCE A

1. The German Federation is a republic. Supreme power comes from the people.
6. The Federal Government alone has the right to legislate on the following subjects: foreign relations . . . immigration, the organisation of the defence forces, coinage, customs, postal and telegraph services.
20. The representatives [i.e. members of the German Parliament, or Reichstag] are elected by the universal, equal, direct and secret vote of all men and women over the age of 20, according to the method of proportional representation.
41. The President of the Federation is elected by the whole German people.
47. The President has supreme command over the whole defence forces of the country.
48. If a state fails to perform its duties . . . the President may enforce performance with the aid of the armed forces.

    If public order and security are seriously disturbed or endangered within the federation, the President may take all necessary steps to restore them, intervening if necessary with the armed forces. For the said purpose, he may suspend for the

time being . . . the fundamental rights described in articles 114, 115, 117, 118, 123, 124 . . .
53. The President . . . appoints and dismisses the Federal Chancellor and, on the latter's recommendation, the Federal ministers.
54. The Federal Chancellor and ministers need the confidence of the Reichstag for the carrying out of their duties.
109. All Germans are equal before the law.
114. Personal freedom is inviolable. No . . . deprivation of personal liberty . . . is admissable unless authorised by the law.
115. The home of every German is inviolable, and a sanctuary for him.
117. Secrecy of correspondence . . . is inviolable.
118. Every German is entitled within the limits of the general law freely to express his opinions by word of mouth, writing, printing . . . or otherwise.
123. All Germans have the right to assemble, peaceably and unarmed.
124. All Germans have the right to form societies for any object that does not go against the criminal law.

Extracts from the Weimar Constitution.

Proportional representation: Instructions

The voting system used in Weimar Germany was proportional representation.

Your teacher will give you **Worksheet 7** which describes how this and other voting systems work. Fill in the spaces on the worksheet.

The first meeting of the Ministers of the Weimar Republic, 1919.

SOURCE B

Reichstagswahl
Wahlkreis Schleswig-Holstein

1	Sozialdemokratische Partei Deutschlands Schroeder - Luise - Eggerstedt - Richter - Biester	**1** ○
2	Deutschnationale Volkspartei Obersohren - Gerns - Wulfing von Ditten - Soth	**2** ○
3	Zentrum Bruning - Hufner - Fuchs, Hedwig - Germeshausen	**3** ○
4	Kommunistische Partei Thulmann - Augustabt, Elise - Heud - Rohre	**4** ○
5	Deutsche Volkspartie Dr. Scifferer - Filcher - Simbal, Elisabeth - Helms	**5** ○
5a	Christlich-Sociale Volksgemeinschaft Brobersen - Grossdinger - Wagner	**5a** ○
6	Deutsch Staatspartei Baulsen - Dr. Ries-Altenloh, Emille - Apfeld Ohlrogge	**6** ○
7	Reichspartei des Deutschen Mittelstandes (Wirschaftspartei) Roster - Reimers - Musfeldt - Rahler	**7** ○
9	Nationalsozialistische Deutsche Arbeiterpartie (Hitlerbewegung) Fransen - Meher-Quade - Thormahlen - Stamer	**9** ○
10	Bauern u. Landvolkpartie Schleswig-Holstein (Christlich- Nationale Bauern und Landvolkpartie) Roster - Reimers - Musfeldt - Rahler	**10** ○
11a	Volksrechtpartei (Reichspartei fur Volksrecht und Rufwertung) und Christlich-Sociale Reichspartei Graf Bosabolveth-Werner - Fied - Henniger - Ruschert	**11a** ○
11b	Volksrechtpartei Merle - Mohr - Richter - Roespei	**11b** ○
12	Deutsche Baurnpartei Leu - Wulff - Harenberg - Woser	**12** ○
16	Treviranus-Konservative Volkspartei Treviranus - Lambach - Rieger - von Uhlerfeld	**16** ○
17	Christlich-Socialer Volksdienst Matthiesen - Thiesen - Buntjen - Stolze	**17** ○
19a	Polnische Volkspartei Lediwolorz - launiezaf - Zhdor - Riwlienletwell	**19a** ○
19b	Schleswigscher Verein Edgaard - Petersen - Elper - Lassen	**19b** ○
19c	Friesland Oldsen - Henningsen - Petersen - Lorenzen	**19c** ○
23	Unabhangige Sozialedemokratishe Partei Deutschlands Liebnecht - Wiegmann, Elsa - Helder - Schroder	**23** ○
24	Haus und Grundbesitzer Webner - Kohlmorgen - Krabad - Schramm	**24** ○
28	Menschheitspartei und Neue Volksgemeinschaft Behdor - Reimpell - Thiel - Duus	**28** ○

A ballot paper from the 1930 Reichstag election.

Friedrich Ebert, First President of the Weimar Republic, 1919–25.

Gustav Stresemann, Foreign Minister of the Weimar Republic, 1923–29

Translation of Source B

Reichstag Election
Electoral District of Schleswig-Holstein

1. Social Democratic Party of Germany
2. German National People's Party
3. Center Party
4. Communist Party
5. German People's Party
5a. Christian-Social National Community
6. German State Party
7. National Party of the German Middle Class (Economic Party)
9. National Socialist German Workers' Party (Hitler Movement)
10. Peasant and Farmfolk Party of Schleswig-Holstein
11a. People's Rights Party (National Party for People's Rights and Revaluation) and National Christian-Social Party
11b. People's Rights Party
12. German Farmers' Party
16. Treviranus-Conservative People's Party
17. Christian-Social National Service
19a. Polish People's Party
19b. Schleswig League
19c. Friesland
23. Independent Social Democratic Party of Germany
24. Landlords and Real Estate Owners
28. Party of Mankind and New National Community

SOURCE C

. . . National Socialism was a revulsion by my friends against parliamentary politics, parliamentary debate, parliamentary government – against all the higgling and haggling of the parties and the splinter parties, their coalitions, their confusions, and their conniving. It was the final fruit of the common man's repudiation of 'the rascals.' Its motif was, 'Throw them all out.' My friends, in the 1920's, were like spectators at a wrestling match who suspect that beneath all the grunts and groans, the struggle and the sweat, the match is 'fixed,' that the performers are only pretending to put on a fight. The scandals that rocked the country, as one party or cabal 'exposed' another, dismayed and then disgusted my friends . . .

Milton Mayer, in The Nazi Years, *edited by J. Remak.*

Questions

Look at Source B.

6 How many parties stood in the 1930 election in this electoral district?

7 What was Party Number 9?

8 What is one of the main effects of the system of proportional representation on the number of political parties standing in an election?

9 Does this system produce:
(a) a fair system;
(b) an efficient system?
Explain your answer.

10 Why were there so many coalitions in the Reichstag during the period 1919–34?

11 How does proportional representation help an unknown party to become powerful?

Look at Source C.

12 What criticisms does the writer make of German politics in the 1920s?

13 How does he explain the success of the Nazi party?

14 Do you agree with his judgement? Explain your answer.

INVASION OF THE RUHR, 1923

Questions

Look at Source A.

1 Who do the children represent? What are the soldiers doing?

Look at Source B.

2 What does the figure represent? What is she doing?

Compare Sources A and B.

3 What are the artists trying to make you feel about (a) Germany and (b) France?

Look at Source C.

4 Explain what Source C shows about the value of the Mark. Explain the changes from 1922 to 1923.

Look at Sources D and E.

5 What effects did these changes have on German life?

6 Which people were most affected?

7 How did these events affect the Germans' opinions of the Weimar Government?

After the war there were many shortages. To make matters worse, prices rose steadily and the Mark came to be worth less and less. Inflation became so bad in 1923 that workers had to be paid daily and then rush to the shops to buy their food at once before the prices shot up again. People's savings became worthless.

When the German government stopped paying reparations in 1923, the French decided to invade the Ruhr, the main German industrial area. The French tried to make the Germans work for them, but the German government ordered a campaign of passive resistance.

SOURCE A

German cartoon, 1923.

SOURCE B

German poster. The caption reads 'Hands off the Ruhr!'

SOURCE C

Number of paper marks for each gold Mark

January	1922	48
July	1922	1,750
May	1923	16,556
August	1923	2,453,595
October	1923	1,205,358,227
November	1923	over 40,000,000,000

SOURCE D

This German shopkeeper had to keep his money in a large box.

Questions

Your character

8 Consider Parts A and B of the character brief you have been given on pages 30 and 31. How does your character feel about the events of 1923? Explain any criticisms you may have of the government or anything you want to say in its defence. Do you think the government has performed well over (a) the inflation and (b) the invasion of the Ruhr?

9 After your discussion write a paragraph explaining whether you think the Weimar Government was a strong and popular government in 1923.

SOURCE E

German children play with worthless money, 1923.

NAZI IDEAS

Look at Source A.

1 What prison was Hitler in when he wrote this letter?

2 Why was he there?

3 What was Nazi policy before 1923?

4 What new policy is Hitler suggesting the Nazis should adopt?

5 Look at the list below. It shows possible Nazi actions. Look at each policy and decide how important it would be for the Nazis:
(a) in 1923 and
(b) after 1923.
Give each policy a mark out of five for each date: five if it was very important and one if it was not important, or any mark in between.

(i)   Buying guns.
(ii)   Making radio broadcasts.
(iii) Organising mass meetings and rallies.
(iv) Paying thugs to beat up enemies of the Nazis, such as communists.
(v)   Holding secret meetings.
(vi) Getting support in the army and police.
(vii) Offering solutions to economic problems.
(viii) Printing posters.
(ix) Getting support from industrialists.
(x)   Winning votes in elections.

In 1921 Hitler became the leader of the National Socialist German Workers Party (Nazis). This party despised the Weimar Republic and were determined to overthrow it by revolution.

In November 1923 the Nazis tried to overthrow the government of Bavaria in the 'Munich Putsch'. Their attempt failed. Hitler was arrested and imprisoned in the Landsberg prison. While in prison he wrote his book, *Mein Kampf* in which he laid out many of his ideas.

Members of the Nazi Party, Munich, 1923: some of Hitler's first followers.

SOURCE A

When I resume active work, it will be necessary to pursue a new policy. Instead of working to achieve power by an armed coup, we will have to hold our noses and enter the Reichstag against the Catholic and Marxist members. If out-voting them takes longer than out-shooting them, at least the result will be guaranteed by their own constitution. Any lawful process is slow – soon we will have a majority and after that – Germany!

An extract from Mein Kampf, *written in prison in 1923.*

SOURCE B

1. We demand the union of all Germans . . . to form a Great Germany.
2. We demand equality of rights for the German People in its dealings with other nations, and the abolition of the Peace Treaty of Versailles.
3. We demand land and territory for the nourishment of our people and for settling our surplus population.
4. None but members of the nation may be members of the State. None but those of German blood . . . may be members of the nation. No Jew, therefore, may be a member of the nation.
6. The right of voting is to be enjoyed by citizens of the State alone . . . all official appointments . . . shall be granted to citizens of the state alone.
8. All further non-German immigration must be prevented.
11. We demand the abolition of incomes unearned by work.
14. We demand that there shall be profit-sharing in the great industries.
15. We demand a generous development of provision for old age.
17. We demand . . . the passing of a law for the confiscation without compensation of land for communal purposes . . . and prohibition of all speculation in land.
18. We demand ruthless war against all whose activities injure the common interest. Common criminals against the nation – money lenders, profiteers etc. – must be punished with death.
19. We demand the education of specially gifted children of poor parents at the expense of the State.
23. . . . We demand that all editors and contributors to newspapers using the German language must be members of the nation . . . that non-Germans be banned from taking part financially in, or influencing, German newspapers.
25. That all these points may be realised, we demand the creation of a strong central government in the Reich.

Some of the 25 points of National Socialism.

SOURCE C

. . . In big things and in small, the movement advocates the principle of the unconditional authority of the leader, coupled with the greatest responsibility . . .

It is one of the supreme tasks of the movement to make this the dominant principle not only for its own ranks, but for the entire state as well.

He who would be a leader shall have the highest, unlimited authority; he also shall bear the final and heaviest responsibility.

He who is not capable of that, or is too cowardly to bear the consequences of his actions, is not fit to be a leader. Only the hero is called . . .

. . . Only when people in Germany will have understood that the German nation's will to life must not wither away in a merely passive defense, only when we have the strength for a final active confrontation with France, and offer a last great decisive battle with some grand German aims indeed, only then will the eternal and basically unfruitful contest between us and France come to an end. What is basic, however, is that Germany truly sees the destruction of France as a means to an end, which is to enable our nation subsequently to expand elsewhere at long last . . .

Extracts from Mein Kampf.

Adolf Hitler, centre stage, 1923.

Questions

Look at Source B.

6 Which of the points are directed against Jews?

7 Which of the points are 'socialist'?

8 Which of the points are 'nationalist'?

Look at Source C.

9 Choose two phrases which show that Hitler believes in strong leadership.

10 Compare Sources B and C. Which of the 25 points agree with the extracts from *Mein Kampf*?

11 How useful are Sources B and C to an historian who wishes to write a balanced account of events in Germany 1919–23?

Your character

12 Choose four of the points in Source B about which your character would have an opinion. Write a paragraph explaining whether your character approves or disapproves of the Nazi policies. Give your reasons.

THE SA

Many Nazis joined the *SA*. These stormtroopers gave impressive evidence of the power of the Nazis.

SOURCE A

SA Poster. The caption reads 'National Race for SA'.

SOURCE B

Photograph of a storm-trooper. The notice reads: 'Germans, stand up for yourselves. Don't buy from Jews.'

SOURCE C *An SA parade.*

Questions

Look at Source A.

1 Describe the uniform of the SA.

2 What impression of the SA is the poster trying to give? How is this effect achieved?

Look at Sources B, C, D and E.

3 Why did the SA appear in public as a 'military formation'?

4 Why did young men join the SA?

5 Describe five ways in which the SA were useful to the Nazis.

Compare *all* the Sources.

6 Which of Sources A–E is Nazi Party propaganda? Explain how you knew.

7 Source E is anti-Nazi. Pick out two incidents which clearly show this. How does Source E disagree with Source D?

Your character

8 Write a paragraph explaining how your character would react to the activities of the SA.

SOURCE D

The only form in which the SA appears to the public is that of the military formation. This is one of the most powerful forms of propaganda. The sight of large numbers of calm, disciplined men whose total will to fight may be seen or sensed, makes the most profound impression on every German... Where whole hosts of men march purposefully, stake life and existence for a cause – that cause must be great and true.

SA leader Franz Pfeffer describes the appeal of the SA.

SOURCE E

There had been a big Nazi meeting at the Sportsplatz... ahead of me were three SA men... All at once they came face to face with a youth of 17 or 18... I heard one of the Nazis shout 'That's him!' and immediately they had jostled him into the shadow of a house entrance and were standing over him, kicking and stabbing with the sharp metal points of their banners... I got a glimpse of his face – his left eye was half poked out and blood poured from the wound... a group of ... heavily armed policemen... disregard the whole affair.

Almost every evening the SA men came into the cafe. Sometimes they were only collecting money – everybody is compelled to give something – sometimes they come to make an 'arrest'. One evening a Jewish writer who was present ran into a telephone box to ring the police. The Nazis dragged him out. Nobody moved a finger. You could have heard a pin drop till they were gone.

An anti-Nazi describes the SA in Goodbye to Berlin *by Christopher Isherwood (1939).*

41

NUREMBERG RALLIES

In order to spread their message the Nazis held huge rallies. Many of these were held in Nuremberg, the centre of their support.

SOURCE A   *The first Nuremberg Rally.*

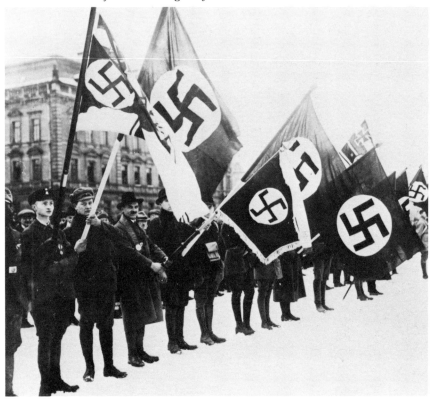

SOURCE B   *The 1929 Rally.*

SOURCE C

The Rally opened on the huge Congress Hall, where 60,000 people gathered to listen to Hitler's proclamation on his achievements of the last three years. Hundreds of swastika banners filed in, to the impressive music . . . and formed a solid mass of red and gold at the back of the stage. Every device of music and coloured lights was used to keep the atmosphere tense and the spotlights played on the giant swastika behind the banners. This exerted an influence that was almost hypnotic.

An eyewitness to a Nuremberg rally.

SOURCE D

'We are strong and will get stronger!' Hitler shouted at them through the microphone. His words echoing across the hushed field through the loudspeakers. And there in the floodlit night jammed together like sardines in one mass formation, the little men of Germany who have made Nazism possible achieved the highest state of being the Germanic man knows – the shedding of their individual souls and minds, until under the magic lights the sound of the magic words of the Austrian merged them completely in the Germanic herd.

An American observer.

SOURCE E

Someone was standing up and had begun to talk, hesitatingly and shyly at first . . . Then suddenly the speech gathered momentum. I was caught, I was listening . . . The crowd began to stir. The haggard faces were reflecting hope . . . Two seats to my left an old officer was crying like a child. I felt alternately hot and cold . . . it was as though guns were thundering . . . I was beside myself. I was shouting. The man up there looked at me for a moment. His blue eyes met my glance like a flame. This was a command. At that moment I was reborn . . . Now I know which way to take.

Goebbels describes the first time he heard Hitler speak.

SOURCE F

Hitler's words were like a whip. When he spoke of the disgrace of Germany I felt ready to spring on any enemy... glancing round, I saw that his magnetism was holding these thousands as one... I was a man of 32, weary with disgust and disillusionment, a wanderer seeking a cause... The intense will of the man, the passion of his sincerity, seemed to flow from him into me. I experienced a feeling that could be likened only to a religious conversion... I felt no-one who heard Hitler that night could doubt he was the man of destiny.

A Nazi describes Hitler speaking.

SOURCE H

German magazine cover from Red Pepper, *a Communist magazine, July 1932.*

SOURCE G

Suddenly military bands break into action... 200 instruments with plenty of trombones and drums – a military march... the party banners appear... and group themselves round the foot of the platform. As they pass through, the crowd... break into a vast shout, 'Heil! Heil! Heil!.'

...And at last the leader, Adolf Hitler. No uniform, just like one of the crowd... Pale tan overcoat, black shoes and socks, black suit and tie, white shirt... Military bands crash out a gigantic salute. Then the leader arises and speaks... One hour, two hours... The crowd hangs on his words... He roars, he pleads: if need be he can weep.

An American journalist describes a Nazi rally in Germany Puts the Clock Back *by Elgar Mowrer.*

Questions

Consider all the sources.

1 Why were Germans depressed and hopeless in 1932?

2 What might Hitler have been saying to give them cause to hope? (Describe at least five topics).

3 Make a list of the methods used by the Nazis to sway the emotions of audiences at rallies.

4 Describe what sort of speaker Hitler was.

5 What do Sources E and F have in common?

6 How can you tell that the writer of Source D is a critic of Hitler?

7 Explain the meaning of Source H. Is it an effective piece of propaganda? Explain your answer.

8 Compare Sources A and B. Explain any differences you can find in the two pictures.

Your character

9 If your character had attended a Nuremberg rally, what reaction would he or she have had? Write a paragraph describing this event.

1929–33

Questions

Look at Source A.

1 Did the Weimar coalition ever have a majority in the Reichstag? What problems did this create?

2 Did the Nazis ever gain a majority in the Reichstag?

3 Which of the five groups shown was most likely to form a coalition with the Nazis in 1933? Explain your answer.

4 Which party lost most support after the 1919 crash? Who gained these votes? Explain why.

5 If the Communists had supported the Weimar coalition after 1929, could they have prevented the Nazis seizing power? Explain your answer.

Look at Source B.

6 What promises is Hitler making?

7 Why might the Germans believe his promises?

8 What sections of German society were most likely to support Hitler?

Look at Source D.

9 Hitler made secret deals with a number of powerful, rich industrialists. They gave him money to pay for his election campaigns. Suggest why they should support him.

Look at Sources A, B and C.

10 Which party grew fastest after the Wall Street Crash? Why do you think this was?

1929 was a bad year for the Weimar Republic. Gustav Stresemann, the respected Chancellor died. Under his leadership, the Weimar government had enjoyed considerable popularity and success during the 1920s.

The Wall Street Crash of 1929 caused the American economy to collapse. German prosperity in the 1920s had been based on American loans. When these were called in, the German economy went into decline. German banks and industries were forced to close. This caused massive unemployment.

The Weimar Government came under severe threat from extremist parties. Between 1929 and 1933 there were a number of elections but no one party was able to rule successfully. Coalitions came and went so governments relied increasingly on the President, Hindenburg, who used his powers to rule by decree.

Between 1929 and 1933, the Nazis made great gains in elections. By 1933, they were the largest party in the Reichstag and so Hindenburg appointed Hitler as Chancellor.

Hitler immediately called another election. He used the state radio to spread his message and flew round Germany whipping up support. Violence flared on the street.

One week before polling began, the Reichstag burned down. Several Communists were accused and Hitler claimed that this was the start of a communist revolution. He used it as an excuse to arrest all his opponents.

When the election results came in, the Nazis had not managed to gain an overall majority. But Hitler took stormtroopers into the Parliament and frightened the members into passing an Enabling Act. This gave Hitler the power to rule without the Reichstag for four years.

In 1934 when Hindenburg died, Hitler became Führer of Germany.

SOURCE A *Election results 1920-33.*

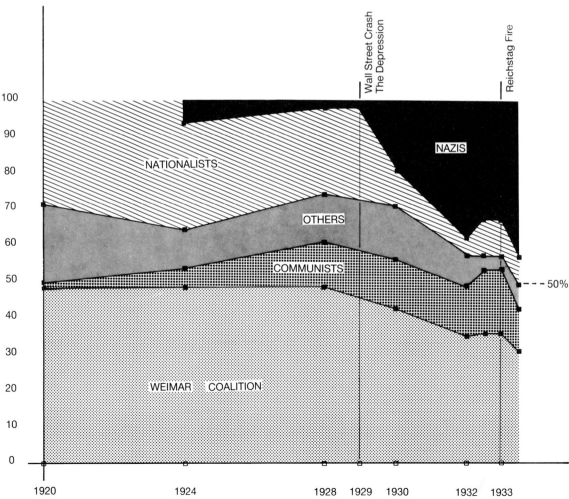

A Nazi election poster. It says: 'Our Last Hope: Hitler.'

Unsere letzte Hoffnung:

HITLER

SOURCE B

Magazine cover of 1932. The text says: 'The meaning of the Nazi salute: Millions are backing me. A little man asks for great gifts.'

A-I-Z

DER SINN DES HITLERGRUSSES:

Kleiner Mann bittet um große Gaben

SOURCE D

. . . The National Socialist movement, assembled, at this hour, as a fighting squad around its leader, today calls on the entire German people to join its ranks, and to pave a path that will bring Adolf Hitler to the head of the nation, and thus

Lead Germany to Freedom

Hitler   Is the password of all who believe in Germany's resurrection.

Hitler   Is the last hope of those who were deprived of everything: of farm and home, of savings, employment, survival, and who have but one possession left: their faith in a just Germany which will once again grant to its citizens honor, freedom, and bread.

Hitler   Is the word of deliverance for millions, for they are in despair, and see only in this name a path to new life and creativity.

Hitler   was bequeathed the legacy of the two million dead comrades of the World War, who died not for the present system of the gradual destruction of our nation, but for Germany's future.

Hitler   Is the man of the people hated by the enemy because he understands the people and fights for the people.

Hitler   Is the furious will of Germany's youth, which, in the midst of a tired generation, is fighting for new forms, and neither can nor will abandon its faith in a better German future. Hence Hitler is the password and the flaming signal of all who wish for a German future.

All of them on March 13, will call out to the men of the old system who promised them freedom and dignity, and delivered stones and words instead: We have known enough of you. Now you are to know us!

SOURCE C   *Nazi propaganda.*

ELECTION RESULTS

Questions

1 Draw a line graph to show the sets of figures in Tables 1 and 2. Mark in the date of the Wall Street Crash and the date when Hitler become Chancellor.

2 What conclusion do you think the Nazi leaders would have drawn from this graph?

3 Draw a bar graph to represent the figures in the table of election results.

Nazi votes and unemployment figures

1928	800,000
1929	6,400,000
July 1932	13,700,000
November 1932	11,700,000

1 Nazi votes.

1929	1,320,000
1930	3,000,000
1931	4,350,000
January 1932	6,000,000
September 1932	5,102,000

2 Unemployment figures.

Election results 1932–33

Party	Number of seats	
	November 1932	March 1933
Nazis	196	233
Nationalists	51	53
People's Party	31	21
Catholic Centre	70	73
Socialists	121	120
Communists	100	81

Election scenes in Berlin, 1929.

Hitler and Hindenburg.

Hitler speaking in the Presidential Election, 1932.

Three German Parties

Party A

This party believes that the whole structure of German life is rotten. The war was caused by greedy, rich men who wanted more power and wealth. But the people who did the suffering were the poor. This state of affairs has not changed since the war. The rich are still rich and the poor are practically starving.

Party A stands for fair shares for all. Everybody is entitled to a decent life and the rich must be made to share out the money they have stolen, and are still stealing, from the poor.

Quarrels between countries will have to stop because they are only quarrels between the rich rulers of different countries. All the poor in all the different countries should join together and fight the rich rather than fight each other.

Party B

This party does not want any more trouble. It has accepted that Germany has lost the war and now wishes to move on from there. Its members believe that the best chance of recovery for Germany is through co-operation and friendship with the other countries of Europe. In this way it will be possible to borrow money from the richer countries to help German recovery.

In order to gain wide support inside Germany, this party tries to be as fair as it can by trying to listen to everybody's point of view.

This party has accepted the Treaty of Versailles, unpleasant though it is, because it considers that if it rejects the Treaty, the rest of Europe will become angry and unfriendly. This might lead to a war that Germany would obviously lose.

Party C

This party is committed to making Germany great again. In the long run the party intends to reverse the Treaty of Versailles which it considers was extremely unfair to Germany. All lands lost in the treaty of Versailles must be returned to Germany.

In order to achieve this the rest of Europe must be convinced that Germany means business. The German armed forces must be increased so that Europe will have to take notice of German wishes.

Germany itself must be united behind a strong leader. Germans must be given a sense of purpose and feel that they are all moving forward together. Listening to everyone's point of view will no longer be a practical proposition because this may divide Germans. The strong leader will take all the decisions and everyone will be glad to follow his advice.

Events in Germany, 1919–34

Dates	What was happening then?
1919	Germany has just lost the war. Revolution in Berlin.
1923	Germany has signed the humiliating Treaty of Versailles. The Mark has gone mad. Many people are ruined. An unknown man, Hitler, has tried to start a revolution in Munich, and has been imprisoned.
1925	Europe starts to accept the Weimar Government. Treaties signed with France, Britain and in 1926, the USSR. Stresemann a respected politician. Hitler out of jail. Has just written *Mein Kampf*.
1929	Wall Street Crash. Massive unemployment and poverty. Stresemann dies. Nazis begin demonstrations and violent election campaigns demanding a new approach to the German problem.
1932	Nazis make massive gains in elections. Thousands flock to join them.
1934	Hitler makes himself Führer. Nazis begin to hunt down opponents. People who stand in their way are imprisoned or shot. Nazis control all radio, newspapers and books. It becomes impossible to hear anything but the Nazi message.

Questions

4 Would you have advised Hitler in 1932 to:
(a) form a coalition with the Nationalist Party;
(b) accept the post of Vice-Chancellor;
(c) wait to be offered the post of Chancellor;
(d) give up elections and start a revolution;
(d) join with all the other parties against the Communists?
Explain your answer.

Look at the descriptions of three German 'parties' on this page.

5 Identify which is:
(a) the Nazi Party;
(b) the Communist Party;
(c) the Social Democrats (Weimar Government).

6 Name two important points of the Nazi Party's policies which are not included in the description.

7 Name two important ways in which the policies of the Nazi Party differed from the policies of the Weimar Government.

Your character

8 Using the descriptions and the summary of events in Germany 1919–1934 to help you, write a paragraph explaining either:
(a) when your character decided to join the Nazi Party; or
(b) why your character did not join the Nazi Party.

9 Write a paragraph describing the hopes and fears of your character in 1934.

THE LONG MARCH

The Background

1911	Chinese Revolution. Nationalists led by Sun Yat-sen overthrow the Manchu Empire. New government based on Sun's 'Three Principles' of Nationalism, Democracy and The People's Livelihood set up in Canton. Second government in Beijing (Peking) led by Yuan Shi-kai who became President backed by the army.
1916	Sun declares war on Germany – Yuan followed in 1917.
1918	Treaty of Versailles allows Japan to keep German territory of Shantung. China gains nothing. China stops buying British and Japanese goods and turns to Russia for friendship. Russia returns land taken from China in the last century. Chinese Communist Party (CCP) begins to grow.
1922	Nationalists or Kuomintang (KMT) fail to defeat powerful warlords. Sun invites CCP to join his army.
1925	Sun Yat-sen dies. Chiang Kai-shek becomes leader of the KMT.
1926	Northern expeditions against warlords are very successful.
1928	Chiang enters Beijing and is accepted as China's new ruler. Chiang believes China needs a strong military leader and decides to get rid of his only rival, the CCP.
1927	Chiang begins a series of attacks on the CCP. KMT death squads hunt down Communists in Canton, killing 6000. Similar attacks in Shanghai and other large cities. Mao Zedong (also called Mao Tse-tung) becomes leader of the CCP. He takes remainder of CCP to the mountains of Kiangsi and sets up a Soviet to rebuild the party and begin a civil war against the KMT.
1931	Chiang begins a series of extermination campaigns to defeat the CCP in Kiangsi. The army of the CCP – Red Army or People's Liberation Army (PLA) – use guerilla tactics. The Japanese invade Manchuria. Chiang decides he must defeat the PLA before turning against the Japanese.

The Long March 1934–5

Read the chart on the left. Chiang spent six years trying to get rid of the Communists and in 1934 he made a final effort to defeat them. He surrounded them in their base at Kiangsi. The CCP was starving and short of ammunition and in April they were badly defeated at Kuangchang.

Mao decided to abandon Kiangsi and take the CCP to the mountains of the north. In October, the Red Army broke through the surrounding KMT forces and began their Long March to safety. They travelled over 6000 miles through dreadful conditions. Of the 400,000 who left Kiangsi, only 4000 reached safety at Yenan.

The following passages are accounts by survivors of the Long March.

The Tatu River

SOURCE A

The army watched breathlessly as the men swung along the bridge chains. Ma Ta-chiu was the first to be shot into the wild torrent below. Then another. The others pushed along, but just before they reached the flooring at the north end of the bridge they saw enemy soldiers dumping cans of kerosene (paraffin) on the planks and setting them on fire.

Watching the last sheet of flame spread, some men hesitated, but the platoon commander sprang down on the flooring before the flames

The Luting Bridge over the Tatu River.

reached his feet, calling to the others to follow. They came and crouched on the planks, releasing their hand grenades and unbuckling their swords. They ran through the flames and threw their hand grenades in the midst of the enemy. More and more men followed, the flames lapping at their clothes. Behind them sounded the roar of their comrades, and beneath the roar the heavy thud, thud, thud of the last tree trunks falling into place. The bridge became a mass of running men with rifles ready.

The Great Snow Mountain

SOURCE B

As we climbed higher and higher we were caught in a terrible hailstorm and the air became so thin that we could scarcely breathe at all. Speech was completely impossible and the cold so dreadful that our breath froze and our hands and lips turned blue.

Men and animals staggered and fell into chasms, and disappeared forever. Those who sat down to rest or relieve themselves froze to death on the spot . . . By nightfall we had crossed, at an altitude of 16,000 feet. To avoid enemy bombers, we arose at midnight and began climbing the next peak. It rained, then snowed, and the fierce wind whipped our bodies and more men died.

The Red Army crosses the Great Snow Mountain during the Long March.

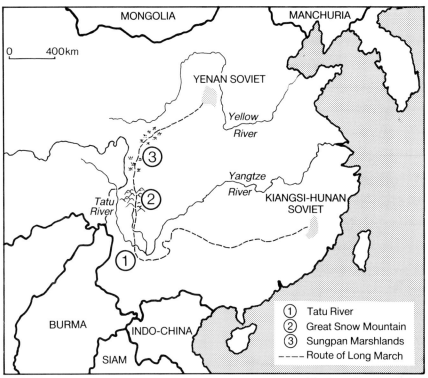

The Long March, 1934-5.

The Sungpan Marshlands

SOURCE C

Treacherous bogs were everywhere which sucked a man down once he stepped off the firmer parts, and more quickly if he tried to pull himself out. We could only advance with great care, stepping on grass clumps . . . It was really like crossing a quicksand. Fortunately the advance guard had left a coarse rope which wandered into the middle of the swamp.

Importance of the Long March

1 It ensured the survival of the Chinese Communists.
2 It ensured Mao's place as 'supreme leader and father figure'.
3 It became a legend and made the Red Army into heroes.
4 While the Red Army was based in Yenan in the north the CCP could always claim they were fighting the Japanese.
5 Chiang had failed to stamp out the main threat to his power.
6 The Red Army took the ideas of communism into every village they visited, and spread Communism among the peasants.

THE LONG MARCH: EXERCISES

Chiang Kai-shek.

SOURCE A

Five times Chiang tried to encircle the Communist or 'Red' area... When Chiang tried to crush them for the fifth time, they broke out of the encircling ring of KMT troops, and on the 16th October 1934 moved away from their base towards the south–west.

Desmond Painter, Mao Tse-tung *(1976).*

SOURCE B *China, 1935.*

① Tatu River
② Great Snow Mountain
③ Sungpan Marshlands
- - - - Route of Long March

SOURCE C

We say that the Long March is the first of its kind ever recorded in history . . . For twelve months we were under daily reconnaissance and bombing from the air by scores of planes. We were encircled, pursued, obstructed and intercepted on the ground by a big force of several hundred thousand men. We encountered difficulties and great obstacles on the way, but by keeping our two feet going we swept across a distance of more than 20,000 li through the length and breadth of eleven provinces.

Well, has there ever been in history a long march like ours? No, never. The Long March is also a manifesto. It proclaims to the world that the Red Army is an army of heroes and that the imperialists and their jackals, Chiang Kai-shek and his like, are perfect nonentities.

The Long March is also an agitation corps. It declares to the two hundred million people of eleven provinces that only the road of the Red Army leads to their liberation. Without the Long March, how could the broad masses have known so quickly that there are such great ideas in the world as upheld by the Red Army?

The Long March is also a seeding-machine. It has sown many seeds in eleven provinces, which will sprout, grow leaves, blossom into flowers, bear fruit and yield a crop in future. To sum up, the Long March ended with our victory and the enemy's defeat.

Mao's view of the importance of the Long March in Chinese communist history. Taken from The Selected Works of Mao Tse-tung *(Vol. 1).*

Mao Zedong.

SOURCE D

Painting of the Long March. Is it a realistic picture or propaganda? Give your reasons.

Questions

1 (a) Describe the events leading up to the Long March 1933–5.

(b) What major difficulties faced the Communists on the Long March?

(c) What does Mao Zedong claim in Source C was achieved by the Long March? What other achievements were made?

(d) What criticisms would you make of Sources A and C as accurate records of the Long March?

2 (a) *Either* Write an account of the Long March remembering to include reasons for it, the difficulties, the length of time of the march and its significance; *or*

(b) Write an account as a journalist reporting for *The Times*. You could have been part of the March or use interviews from survivors. To help you, read the accounts of the March on pages 48–9. Don't forget to give background material. Bring out the character of Mao if you can. A good headline always helps.

3 Write a short essay on the Long March under the following paragraph headings:
(a) the plan
(b) the escape
(c) crossing the Tatu River
(d) the Great Snow Mountain
(e) the Sungpan Marshes
(f) arrival at Yenan.

Look at Source D, and other pictures of Mao in this chapter.

4 (a) What impression does Source D give of Mao?

(b) Is this the same as the impression given by other pictures?

(c) Explain any differences between them.

LIFE IN YENAN

SOURCE A   *Yenan: Headquarters of Mao's forces.*

Between 1937 and 1942, Mao created a new society in Yenan using ideas he had tried out in Kiangsi. Many of the people lived in caves cut in the soft rock.

Life was based on co-operation between the peasants and the soldiers. When peasants harvested, soldiers helped. When soldiers dug gun pits, peasants helped. General Peng Te-huai said: 'The people are the water, the soldiers of the 8th Route Army are the fish. The fish cannot live without the water.' Peasants became soldiers and/or provided food and labour.

Both men and women played an equal part in this society. Women fought alongside men. Men spun cotton alongside women. Both took responsibility on the Peasant Associations.

Decision-making was shared by peasants and soldiers through elected committees.

Peasants began to invent their own songs and dances while Mao began to develop his own philosophy. He based his ideas on Marx and Lenin but applied it to China. What resulted was known as 'Maoism'.

Maoism

Lenin saw the town workers (urban proletariat) as the main revolutionary force in Russia.

Since there were few industrial workers in China, Mao saw the country peasants as the main revolutionary force.

Mao said that no one must stray from the path of revolution. Each peasant must watch out for his/her political shortcomings. There had to be a continual process of self-criticism and self-improvement.

SOURCE C

Everyone carried a weapon of some sort – a rifle on his back, a grenade at his hip . . . even the little boys and girls wore dummy grenades dangling from their waists.

Written by an American journalist.

SOURCE B   *Mao at Yenan, 1938.*

Questions

1 Why did Mao go to Yenan?

2 Look at the photograph of Yenan (Source A). Give two reasons why it was such a good base for Mao.

3 Explain the purpose of the 'cave university'.

4 Explain the main differences between the ideas of Lenin and Mao.

5 Can you find any other evidence on these pages to support the American journalist's statement (Source C)? How useful is his evidence?

SOURCE D *Students at the cave university, Yenan.*

Mao taught his ideas along with other leaders to thousands of Red Army recruits at Yenan. His lectures and essays at the 'cave university' became the basis of what was known eventually as the *Thoughts of Chairman Mao*. People who visited saw his ideas put into practice. However, it is important to remember that life in Yenan was often harsh, often a struggle. Conditions remained primitive and people had to learn to live with a constant war situation. Disease and malnutrition were always present.

*Members of the Friends' Ambulance Unit treating a Chinese soldier. The Quakers were among the few Westerners allowed into Yenan. (Use this picture with **Worksheet 9**).*

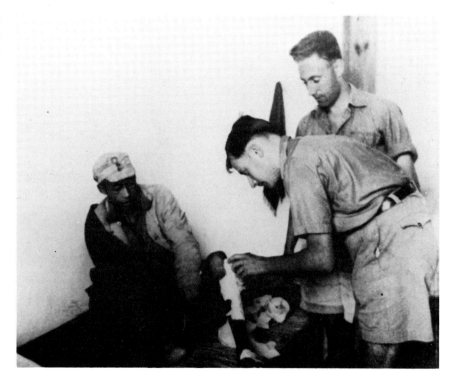

53

GUERILLA WARFARE

Mao knew that the Red Army would be smashed if it fought battles with the Kuomintang which had modern equipment. So he taught his soldiers the techniques of guerilla warfare. Most of the time the Red Army was invisible. The soldiers became ordinary peasants, working in the field. They only came together when they were sure of winning a battle. Below you will find a selection of the rules made about guerilla fighting. They have been copied by every guerilla army in the world.

The enemy attacks, we retreat;
The enemy camps, we raid;
The enemy tires, we attack;
The enemy retreats, we pursue.

How Mao thought the war should be fought

'With our tactics the masses can be aroused for struggle on an ever-broadening front, and no enemy, however, powerful can cope with us. Ours are guerilla tactics. They consist of the following points.

Divide our forces to arouse the masses; concentrate our forces to deal with the enemy. To extend stable base areas, employ the policy of advancing in waves; when pursued by a powerful enemy, employ the policy of circling round behind.

Arouse the largest numbers of masses in the shortest possible time and by the best possible methods.

The tactics are just like casting a net. At any moment we should be able to cast it or draw it in. We cast it wide to run over the masses, and draw it in to deal with the enemy.'

Guerilla warfare according to Peng Teh-huai, Commander of the 1st Front Red Army

1 Partisans must not fight any losing battles. Do not fight if you are not sure of winning.
2 Surprise is the main weapon. Keep moving.
3 A careful and detailed plan of attack and especially retreat must be worked out before a battle.
4 The partisans must always outnumber the enemy in a battle. Attack in strength where the enemy is weakest or most unprepared.
5 Do not fight the main enemy army but concentrate on their weakest links.
6 Get as much information as you can from your friends, the masses (peasants). Make use of your superior knowledge.
7 It is absolutely necessary for the partisans to win the support and participation of the peasant masses. If there is no movement of armed peasants there is no base for the partisans and the Red Army cannot exist.

Military principles of the People's Liberation Army

1 Attack scattered, isolated enemy forces first; attack concentrated, strong enemy forces later.
2 Take the country areas first. Take small cities later and large cities last of all.
3 The main aim is to wipe out the enemy's army. It is not to capture or hold strong enemy positions. These positions can be taken after the enemy's army has been wiped out.
4 Fight no battle unprepared. Fight no battle you are not sure of winning.
5 Keep moving.
6 Build up your strength with captured weapons. Win over enemy soldiers to your side.

The 8th Route Army helps to train and organise peasants.

Instructions

You are Mao's right hand person. You have been given the task of writing down the rules of the Red Army. Choose only six from the list below and write them down. Make sure they fit into Mao's ideas of how guerilla wars should be fought. Then answer the questions.

1 Stand no nonsense from the peasants.
2 Take what you want from anyone.
3 Return all borrowed articles.
4 Do not pay for what you can steal.
5 Replace all damaged articles.
6 Persuade the peasants to support the KMT.
7 Be courteous and polite to people and help them whenever you can.
8 Show no mercy to peasants who do not help.
9 Be honest in all your dealings with the peasants.
10 Pay for all goods you buy from peasants.
11 Force peasants to join the Red Army.
12 Be clean and sanitary and dig lavatories at a safe distance from the village.
13 Leave houses as you found them.
14 Burn peasants houses you have slept in to destroy evidence of your stay.
15 Do not give weapons to the peasants, they cannot be trusted.
16 Do not hesitate to torture peasants for information.
17 Shoot all KMT prisoners to make them fear the Red Army.
18 Do not talk to peasants if you can help it.

Questions

1 Explain why you chose the six rules you did.

2 Select four of the rules you did not choose and explain exactly why you left them off your list.

3 Explain who partisans were.

4 Write a short account of Red Army tactics. Explain why the peasants supported the PLA and why Chiang's army lost support.

GUERILLA WARFARE: EXERCISES

Questions

1 Explain what you could do for the villagers and what the villagers could do for you.

2 Explain what you would do in each of the following situations.
(a) A small KMT force is operating 10 miles away from the village.
(b) A large well-equipped KMT army is advancing towards the village.
(c) A rich landlord complains that a peasant has not paid her rent.
(d) Four KMT deserters arrive at the village asking for shelter.
(e) A cartload of PLA arms and ammunition is sent to the village.

3 The peasants who live in Ling Po want to help your PLA unit. List the ways in which they can do this. Here are some clues to help you.
(a) They know the area very well.
(b) They can travel short distances from the village without arousing suspicion.
(c) Only they know who lives in the village.
(d) They have many practical skills.

4 Why might children and women play a specially useful role in supporting a guerilla unit?

5 KMT units generally live in fortified areas in towns. What advantages does this give your PLA unit?

6 Why do you think the name People's Liberation Army was chosen?

7 Which do you think is the most important rule of guerilla fighting? Explain your choice.

Instructions

Imagine you are in command of a small group of Red Army fighters. You have arrived at the village of Ling Po. The plan of the village is shown below. Your fighters have some expert knowledge of the following: fighting, medicine, farming, engineering, Communist ideas. You are all fit and healthy. You can all read and write.

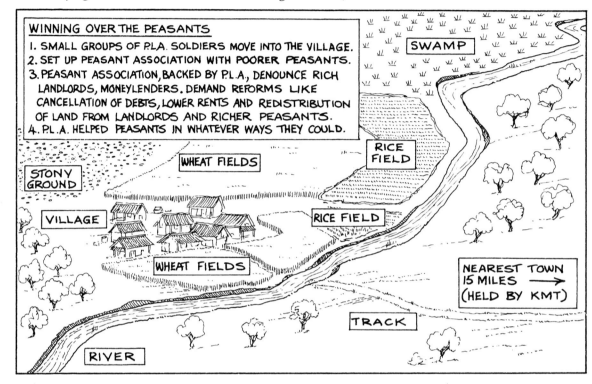

WINNING OVER THE PEASANTS
1. SMALL GROUPS OF P.L.A. SOLDIERS MOVE INTO THE VILLAGE.
2. SET UP PEASANT ASSOCIATION WITH POORER PEASANTS.
3. PEASANT ASSOCIATION, BACKED BY P.L.A., DENOUNCE RICH LANDLORDS, MONEYLENDERS. DEMAND REFORMS LIKE CANCELLATION OF DEBTS, LOWER RENTS AND REDISTRIBUTION OF LAND FROM LANDLORDS AND RICHER PEASANTS.
4. P.L.A. HELPED PEASANTS IN WHATEVER WAYS THEY COULD.

SWAMP · RICE FIELD · WHEAT FIELDS · STONY GROUND · VILLAGE · RICE FIELD · WHEAT FIELDS · NEAREST TOWN 15 MILES → (HELD BY KMT) · TRACK · RIVER

Ling Po. The village has no water supply, doctor or school. The infant death rate is very high. None of the villagers can read or write. The huts are wooden with thatched roofs. The swamp is unhealthy. Cultivation methods are primitive. Flour is ground by hand. The villagers keep a few pigs and chickens. Ling Po is regularly raided by KMT soldiers who loot, burn and rape. Most of the land is owned by three rich landlords.

Peasants transport food to the Communist front line.

Instructions

Read Sources A–E and answer the questions on this page and question 4 on **Worksheet 10**.

SOURCE A

The Generalissimo has personally come to save you . . . Only the brigand leaders, Chuh Teh and Mao Tse-tung will be killed . . . rise up quickly and kill all the red brigands in order to regain your freedom. Brigand soldiers come quickly to join the Revolutionary Army. Each brigand soldier who comes with a rifle will be rewarded. Red brigands are mean and low.

A Chinese leaflet written in 1932.

SOURCE B

Political power grows out of the barrel of a gun.

Mao Zedong.

SOURCE C

The enemy attacks, we retreat;
The enemy camps, we raid;
The enemy tries, we attack;
The enemy retreats, we pursue.

Mao Zedong.

SOURCE D

The People's Liberation Army is like a net.

Mao Zedong.

SOURCE E

1 Speak politely to the people and help them whenever you can.
2 Return doors and straw matting to the owners.
3 Pay for any damage you cause.
4 Pay a fair price for any goods you buy.
5 Be sanitary – establish latrines well away from houses.
6 Don't take liberties with the womenfolk.
7 Don't ill-treat prisoners.
8 Don't damage crops.

The eight rules of the 8th Route Army.

Battle-scarred veteran of the 8th Route Army.

A Red Army guerilla on guard near the paddy fields.

Questions

8 Look at Source A.

(a) Who was the 'Generalissimo'?

(b) Who were the 'brigand soldiers'?

(c) What was the 'Revolutionary Army' mentioned in the leaflet?

(d) What was the purpose of the leaflet?

(e) What is the name given to this type of statement?

(f) How effective do you think this leaflet was? Give as many reasons as you can to explain why it was likely or unlikely to succeed?

WAR AGAINST THE JAPANESE

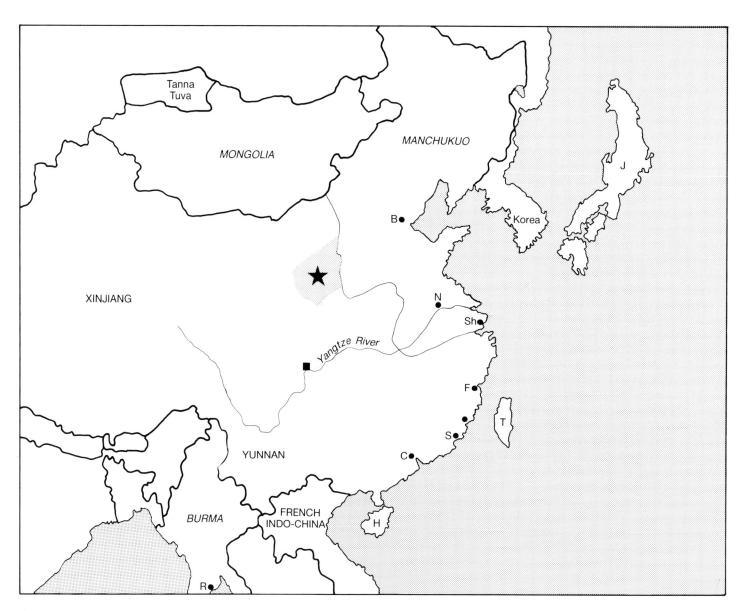

*The situation in China, 1940. Use this map with **Worksheet 10**.*

Questions

1 Why did the Japanese find it hard to defeat the PLA?

2 The Japanese hit back with reprisals (taking hostages and executing them). What effect do you think this had on recruitment for the PLA?

3 Much of the time the Japanese took no action against the PLA. How did Mao use these periods of rest to help the PLA?

The Japanese invaded Manchuria in 1931. Japan had fought many wars with China in the past and had always had ambitions to own an empire on the mainland. Manchuria contained many natural resources such as coal and oil.

Once Manchuria had been conquered the Japanese changed its name to Manchukuo and placed the Chinese former child-Emperor, Pu Yi on the throne of this puppet state.

In spite of this invasion, Chiang refused to join the CCP in fighting their common enemy and continued with the civil war. It was not until 1937 that Chiang agreed to ally with the CCP and form a United Front. The Japanese, fearing a united China, invaded the rest of the country in 1937.

The Japanese had a powerful, well-equipped army supported by a modern airforce. They were brutal in attacks, ruthlessly bombing large cities like Nanking. Within a year the KMT had been defeated and Chiang took refuge in the mountain city of Chungking. Only the PLA continued to fight with any vigour, launching the 'Hundred Regiments Campaign' in 1940.

In 1941, the Japanese attacked Pearl Harbor and the USA entered the war. The American government sent supplies to the KMT in Chungking along the Burma Road and by air.

The PLA fights the Japanese

At first the Japanese thought of the PLA simply as bandits who were a nuisance but not a serious threat. But it soon became clear that the 'bandits' controlled large areas of what was supposed to be Japanese-occupied territory. The Japanese, realising that the PLA needed the support of the peasants, launched a bloody campaign against the villages called the 'Three Alls' – kill all, burn all, destroy all. The PLA were forced into the mountains or, literally, underground.

Japanese troops posing for a photograph in the streets of Mukden, 1931.

SOURCE A

We worked during the day and dug tunnels at night. By the beginning of 1945 we had completed four main tunnels with 24 branches radiating out from them. We also dug more than 15 kilometres of tunnels to connect us with neighbouring villages. Our tunnels not only had direction signs and oil lamps at the turns, but we had rest places, food stores, kitchens and latrines. The entrances were usually at the base of a wall under brick beds or in dry wells. Inside the entrance we made the tunnel dip down and up again . . . if the enemy pumped in poison gas we blocked the caves with earth so the gas couldn't get in.

A member of the PLA remembers.

Japanese troops attacking a Nationalist base, 1939.

Chinese underground tunnels.

In 1942 the Japanese began building blockhouses (forts). Operating from these they began to clear villages. Villages were surrounded by wattel fences and then anyone inside suspected of being a Communist was killed and the other peasants driven away.

By August, 1500 blockhouses had been built and 8000 villages cleared. Mao then took a terrible revenge. The 8th Route Army was placed near villages and waited until the end of the long dry season. At the beginning of September, hundreds of miles of fencing was set alight and thousands of Japanese were roasted in their own traps.

THE COMMUNIST VICTORY

Questions

1 What do you think Mao meant when he described the Atom bomb as a 'paper tiger'?

2 What evidence can you think of that proves this argument that weapons do not decide everything, but that people do?

3 Can you think of any reasons why Mao was not frightened of the atom bomb?

4 Why was the American government suspicious of the CCP?

On 6 August 1945, the USA dropped an atomic bomb on Japan. Another followed a few days later. On 8 August Stalin invaded Manchuria. Within a week the Japanese surrendered.

Mao commented on the A-bomb:

'Can atom bombs decide wars? No they can't. Atom bombs could not make Japan surrender. Without the struggles waged by people atom bombs could be of no avail. The atom bomb is a paper tiger.' (*The Selected Works of Mao Zedong*)

The American government, suspicious of the CCP, ordered the Japanese to surrender only to the KMT and continued to send aid to Chiang. On paper, the KMT looked like the most powerful ruling party in China, but in the eyes of the 100 million peasants of northern China, the CCP were more important.

The civil war continues

With the Japanese threat removed, the civil war began again. At the start in 1946, Chiang had a large, well-equipped army thanks to aid from the USA. He had done little fighting against the Japanese so he still had plenty of equipment.

However, during the war Chiang had lost the support of the peasants and even the Americans felt that his rule was very corrupt. For example, American pilots took great risks flying transport planes over the mountains to bring equipment to

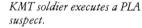
KMT soldier executes a PLA suspect.

The mushroom cloud over Hiroshima.

Chiang. (This was called flying over the 'Hump'.) On one occasion a crate being unloaded broke open and was found to contain hundreds of items of silk underwear for Chiang's wife.

Many Chinese felt that Mao had led the more effective resistance against the Japanese and knew that during the Japanese occupation they had received a lot of practical help from the PLA who controlled most of the countryside. Chiang found that many of his soldiers deserted the KMT rather than fight the Reds.

Civil war 1946-9

The KMT controlled China south of the Yangtse river and held most of the cities in the north and in Manchuria. The Communists controlled the countryside in between, so that contact between the two groups of nationalists had to be by air.

The PLA on the march.

Questions

5 Why did the USA *not* support the PLA?

6 Why did Chiang Kai-shek lose the civil war? You could answer this as a list of reasons or a paragraph or as a full essay.

7 You are a member of the PLA who has been with Mao since the beginning. Write an essay explaining why the Communists were able to take control of China and set up the People's Republic in 1949. You should mention:
(a) the Long March;
(b) Mao's ideas;
(c) Yenan;
(d) guerilla fighting;
(e) the support of the peasants;
(f) mistakes made by the KMT;
(g) any other points you think are important.

Main events of the civil war

June 1946–Spring 1947	Chiang attacks the PLA in Manchuria, promising that the reds would be defeated in six months. USA supplies KMT forces from the air. PLA uses guerilla tactics.
1948	Mao gathers his forces and drives the KMT back into their town bases. Prices in the KMT areas rise steeply and morale is low.
1949 January April–May October December	The PLA captures every major city north of the Yangtse and wins three major battles in Manchuria. Beijing surrenders. Shanghai and Nanking taken. Canton, the last major city held by the Nationalists, surrenders. Chiang Kai-shek takes what is left of his KMT supporters and flees to the island of Taiwan. He remains here as President until his death in 1975.

On 1 October 1949, Mao appeared at the Gate of Heavenly Peace at the Imperial Palace in Beijing. He read a speech which proclaimed the People's Republic of China.·

Celebration of the first anniversary of the People's Republic of China, 1950.

61

PREPARATIONS FOR WAR

At 11.15 a.m. on 3 September 1939, Neville Chamberlain, the Prime Minister announced on BBC Radio:

'I am speaking to you from the Cabinet Room at 10 Downing Street. This morning the British Ambassador in Berlin handed the German government a final note, stating that unless we heard from them by 11 o'clock that they were prepared at once to withdraw their troops from Poland, a state of war would exist between us. I have to tell you now that no such undertaking has been received and that consequently this country is at war with Germany.'

The war did not come as a surprise to most Britons. Since 1933 Hitler had been gaining power in Germany. In March 1938 German soldiers occupied Austria. In March 1939 they marched into Czechoslovakia. Yet the British government and people wanted peace; the memory of World War 1 was still present and so was the memory of the economic hardships which had followed it. There had been great relief when Prime Minister Chamberlain, after a meeting with Hitler in September 1938, had announced that he had secured 'peace in our time'.

But the threat of war could not be ignored and preparations had been going ahead in Britain.

The chief fear was of air attacks, and it was thought that the skies would be impossible to defend. Casualties, especially in large, densely populated cities such as London, would be enormous.

To help deal with the expected destruction at home, the organisation of defence had been improved. From 1935 local authorities had been planning Air Raid Precautions (ARP). The number of volunteer wardens gradually increased although there was much confusion at first as to what was expected of them and what action they should take.

One of the ARP wardens' earliest jobs was to distribute and demonstrate the use of gas masks to people in their area, for it was believed that the dropping of gas would be part of the new war. Thirty-eight million gas masks were issued before war was declared, including 'Mickey Mouse' masks for children. The tops of some pillar boxes were painted with a special gas-detecting paint.

The blacking out of all lights that shone in the street was being started and practised (blackout). The government had begun to draw up plans for moving people out of the towns and into the country (evacuation). This applied particularly to children. Some firms and government departments were also preparing to move from these danger areas.

Any reservists and the Territorial Army had been called up by late August 1939. All over the country, people who remembered shortages of World War 1, had begun to stock up with a few extra provisions 'just in case'.

During the period September 1939 (German invasion of Poland) to April 1940 (German invasion of Norway) Britain did little except prepare for Hitler's attack. There were no air raids or battles. The RAF dropped leaflets on Germany. There was a propaganda battle about the effects of the Blitzkrieg attack on Poland.

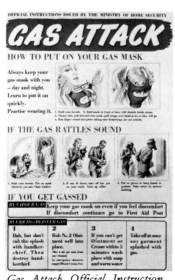

Gas Attack Official Instruction Manual.

The dangers of a gas attack, 1939.

British cartoon, 1939.

In Britain there were air raid practices and blackout was introduced. Cars could not use headlights. As a result there were 3000 deaths from road accidents.

People began to complain. Why go to all the bother and inconvenience of ARP when there was no one to hide from? Neville Chamberlain seemed unwilling to wage effective war. He seemed to think the war was never coming.

The country and Parliament looked for a more effective leader. All the parties seemed to favour Winston Churchill. On 10 May 1940 he became leader of a coalition government. The new tone was set in his first speech. 'I have nothing to offer but blood, toil, tears and sweat.'

British cartoon, 1939, from the Evening Standard.

Local Archive Project: Instructions

Your teacher will issue you with **Resource F**, 'What is a local archive?'

These instructions for the Local Archive Project were issued to fifth-year students at our school. You will be doing the same project, but remember that you should use your local museum or library, and fix up an interview with someone who was there at the time. Your teacher will give you additional instructions and help and the rest of the unit will give you ideas on what sources to look for and where you might find them.

At the end of the project, you will have to produce an exhibit for a local archive. The most common form of exhibit is a display panel (see right) but may also include taped interviews, models, photographs, examples of cookery and films.

NOTE. The display panel may be produced by a group of students. After it is finished, however, each individual will have to complete **Worksheet 13** saying what sources you used, and what you found out about the Home Front. This summary sheet will be marked and may count as part of your GCSE coursework.

Scheme for Display Panel

1 A hardboard panel measuring about 4ft × 2ft 6 inches (120 × 80 cm).
2 Extracts from an interview with an Air Raid Warden in your area.
3 Photograph of German bomber (from text book).
4 Headlines from a local paper published the day after the first air raid.
5 Letraset/artwork for main title.
6 Photo of barrage balloon (from museum).
7 Red tape/arrows.
8 A cover of clear plastic.

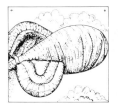

SOURCE JIGSAW

Instructions

Study the ten pieces of evidence shown here and answer the questions on **Worksheet 11** which your teacher will give to you.

1 That most jealously preserved of editorial prerogatives – the right to the last word – is now used to repair an omission. No mention has been made of the womenfolk, whose patience, tolerance and co-operation were essential, yet they, too, made sacrifices and their support is gratefully acknowledged. We hope this little book will confirm their husbands' version of Home Guard service; that they will forgive the spoiled Sunday dinners, the late suppers and the muddy boots. They were long suffering but served us well. We thank them.

2

3

WASTE THE FOOD AND HELP THE HUN

NATIONAL RATIONING.

TRAVELLER'S RATION BOOK R.B.3.

How to use this book.

1. The consumer's name and address must be written (in BLOCK LETTERS) in the space provided on the reference leaf (page III).

Purchases and coupons.

2. Every time you buy rationed food you must hand your ration book to the retailer and he will detach the appropriate coupons. You must not detach coupons yourself. If you do they will be useless.

3. Coupons not used in the week to which they relate cannot be used later.

Meat meals.

4. Half a meat or bacon coupon may be used to obtain a cooked meal of rationed meat or bacon in a hotel, restaurant, café, tea shop, etc. The half coupon must be detached from your ration book by the person serving the meal.

Cooked meat.

5. You may purchase cooked rationed meat at cooked meat shops, but only on surrender of a coupon or half coupon. The coupon or half coupon must be detached from your ration book by the person supplying you.

Spare Coupons.

6. Do nothing with the pages numbered 7, 8 and 9 until told what to do.

Joining the Navy, Army or Air Force.

7. If you join the Navy, Army or Air Force, or are supplied with rations by the Government or other authority, return this book to the Food Office at once.

Leaving Great Britain.

8. If you intend to leave Great Britain for more than four weeks, you must hand this book to an Immigration Officer when you embark. If you are going abroad for a shorter period you may retain it but you must show it to the Immigration Officer on leaving and on your return.

Penalties for misuse.

9. Any false statement, misuse of this book or breach of these instructions renders you liable to a penalty.

Consumer's Name (BLOCK LETTERS)

HER MAJESTY THE QUEEN

Address (BLOCK LETTERS)
BUCKINGHAM PALACE
LONDON. S.W.1. CA 570012

Date 16 January 1940

4 Many women worked in factories. They made guns, aircraft, tanks and munitions. Munitions were the bullets and shells for guns. The work hours were long and hard. A girl would start at 8 a.m. She would finish work at 7 p.m. She might work a long way from home. She might not get home until 8 p.m. or later. Many girls still had the energy to go dancing in the evening. Some factory work was unpleasant. One girl had been working in a dress shop. She was good at sewing. She was sent to an aircraft factory. She sewed linen on to the wings. The aeroplanes were Wellington bombers. She had to sew 70 feet (about 20 metres.)

7

ARP **LOOKS TO YOU**

WOMEN'S VOLUNTARY SERVICES

9

8

The Women of Britain: a Tribute

10

By Canadians

Twelve Canadian newspaper men who, after a six-weeks tour of Britain, are returning to Canada this week, yesterday gave me their views of Britain at war.

Said H.M. Major, news editor of *La Press*, published in Montreal: "It is the women of Britain who particularly stand out in this war. We have seen women of the Red Cross, the Services, and Civil Defence. We have seen them working huge and complicated machines in the factories and stooping to mend roads with a pick and shovel and we find them—magnificent. I cannot praise your women too much."

CARROT CAKE   **6**

INGREDIENTS

8 oz carrots – grated   *½ teaspoon ground*
4 oz mixed dried fruit – as   *cinnamon*
available   *½ teaspoon Bicarb of soda*
7 tablespoons of water   *1 teaspoon Baking powder*
7 tablespoons of oil   *2 eggs slightly beaten or*
4 oz sugar or sweetener/syrup *equivalent egg powder*

METHOD

1 Put carrots, fruit, water, oil, sweetener and salt and spices in a saucepan. Bring to the boil, cook for five minutes. Cool.

2 Add dry ingredients.
Add eggs. Put into lined 2 lb loaf tin. Bake in a moderate oven 350°F, gas mark 4 for an hour. Cool slightly before removing from tin.

THE HOME GUARD

Questions

1 What was the LDV? Why was it set up?

2 What sort of people joined the LDV? Why did they join?

Look at Sources C and D.

3 Comment on the weapons, uniforms and appearance of the members of the LDV shown in these photographs. Why are the LDV equipped in this way?

Look at all the sources.

4 On the basis of these sources alone, do you think the LDV would have been an effective force? Explain your answer.

Sources C–I are placed in chronological order.

5 Use the pictures to explain how the equipment and training of the LDV improved throughout the war.

Using all the sources.

6 Write a short description of a day in the life of a member of the LDV.

The Home Guard, or Local Defence Volunteers, were formed after an appeal by the War Minister.

SOURCE A

We want large numbers of men who are not at present engaged in military service between the ages of seventeen and sixty-five to come forward and offer their services... You will not be paid but you will receive uniform and will be armed.

Anthony Eden, War Minister, in a broadcast on 14 May 1940.

The volunteers were needed for night duties in case of attack by German paratroopers. Over a quarter of a million men joined up on the first day; by June 1940 there were one and a half million men in the Home Guard.

On 22 May 1940, there was a meeting at Torbay police station to form a company of the Local Defence Volunteers. The Company Commander was Lt.-Col. Despard Davies (Indian Army, retired). The Company was divided into four platoons as follows:

Platoons 1 and 2	Torquay
Platoon 3	Paignton
Platoon 4	Brixham

Section 18 of F (Torquay) Company

This section of the Home Guard was formed by 88 volunteers from the Torquay Electricity Company. The section's main job was to guard the electricity sub-stations, but they also spotted enemy aircraft and patrolled other areas of Torquay. One member of the section has provided this brief history of their activities:

SOURCE B

The section had no arms or ammunition when these duties were commenced and the most useful early weapons were pick-axe handles with the heads drilled out to receive a couple of pounds of molton lead. Even after rifles were issued, many of the older and non-military minded members preferred to carry a loaded pick-handle than a firearm during the night's patrol!

One of these men, 60 years of age, was heard one night to challenge, in his Welsh dialect, this: 'I'm afraid I must ask you to stop.'

By July 1st, 1940 the strength of the section has risen to 94, but almost immediately resignations due to call-up began to come in. Seven rifles and 70 rounds were issued to the section this month, enabling sentries to carry five rounds.

At the end of the month, rifles on charge numbered 20 with 400 rounds.

At the end of August, the first denims and steel helmets were issued. By September the first battle dresses and boots had been issued, but it was not until March, 1941, that all ranks were more or less kitted out, with the exception of a few outsize battle dresses and respirators.

In January 1941, serious regular parades and instructions commenced with Sgt. W. F. Hallion and Cpl. F. B. Cowling as instructors, and the platoon, in addition to carrying out its nightly guard duties, managed to send three men per night for four weeks to assist the Newton Abbot Platoon in their guard on the Power Station.

Taken from 'On Guard', edited by G. H. Lidstone, 1945.

SOURCE C
LDV drill.

SOURCE D *'Drainpipe' gun.*

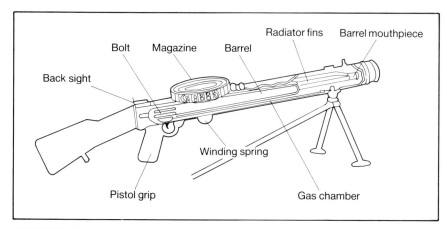

Back sight — Bolt — Magazine — Barrel — Radiator fins — Barrel mouthpiece
Pistol grip — Winding spring — Gas chamber

SOURCE F *Home Guard weapon.*

SOURCE E *Home Guard with rifle.*

SOURCE G

In the event of observing German Parachutists, telephone High Wycombe 26.

Standing Orders of the 4th Battalion, Buckinghamshire LDV, summer 1940.

SOURCE H *LDV gun team.*

SOURCE I *Anti-aircraft gun.*

AIR RAIDS 1942–43

ANOTHER SAVAGE RAID ON EXETER

Widespread Devastation By H.E. and Fire Bombs

HEART OF CITY 'BLITZED'

SOURCE A
Headlines from the Express and Echo, *a local newspaper.*

SOURCE B   *An artist's impression of a German bomber over Exeter.*

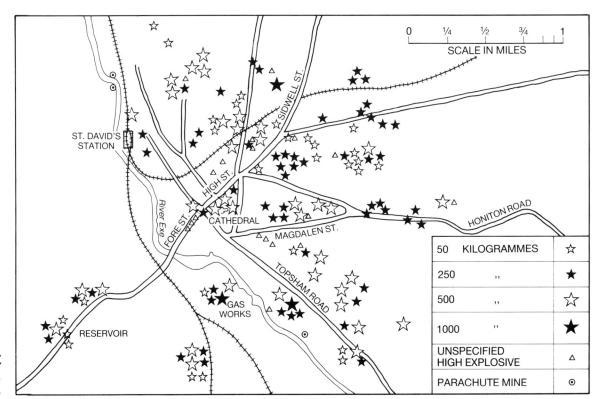

SOURCE C
*The bombing of Exeter,
4 May 1942.*

50	KILOGRAMMES	☆
250	,,	★
500	,,	☆
1000	,,	★
UNSPECIFIED HIGH EXPLOSIVE		△
PARACHUTE MINE		⊙

here's a *man's* job!

SOURCE D   *Government poster.*

Morrison shelters proved their worth over and over again. In one shattered house four children in the family shelter were unscathed, although the shelter was completely buried in debris. In another, where it was feared there fatal casualties, a police officer's shout received a welcome answer–two middle-aged women crawled out of their shelter unhurt and quite cheerful, despite the destruction of their dwelling.

The speed and efficiency with which the rescue and casualty services carried out their tasks made a very favourable and reassuring impression throughout the district. Men worked skilfully and unceasingly until every inhabitant had been accounted for. Almost all the people rendered homeless went to the houses of relations or friends. In accordance with the prearranged scheme, the others were accompanied at a rest centre which was opened promptly by the local authority.

To-day two emergency feeding centres are in operation in the district.

SOURCE F   *Express & Echo, April–May 1942.*

IF WAR SHOULD COME

The object of this leaflet is to tell you now some of the things you ought to know if you are to be ready for the emergency of war.

This does not mean that war is expected now, but it is everyone's duty to be prepared for the possibility of war.

Further leaflets will be sent to you to give you fuller guidance on particular ways in which you can be prepared.

The Government are taking all possible measures for the defence of the country, and have made plans for protecting you and helping you to protect yourselves, so far as may be, in the event of war.

You, in your turn, can help to make those plans work, if you understand them and act in accordance with them.

No-one can tell when or how war might begin, but the period of warning might be very short. There would be no time then to begin to think you ought to do.

READ WHAT FOLLOWS, and think NOW.

(1) AIR RAID WARNINGS

When air raids are threatened, warning will be given in towns by sirens or hooters, which will be sounded, in some places by short blasts, and in other places by a warbling note, changing every few seconds. In war, sirens and hooters will not be used for any other purpose than this.

The warning may also be given by the Police or Air Raid Wardens blowing short blasts on whistles.

When you hear the warning, take cover at once. Remember that most of the injuries in an air raid are caused not by direct hits by bombs, but by flying fragments of debris or bits of shells. Stay under cover until you hear the sirens or hooters sounding continuously for two minutes on the same note, "Raiders Passed".

If poison gas has been used, you will be warned by means of hand rattles. Keep off the streets until the poison gas has been cleared away. Hand bells will be rung when there is no longer any danger. If you hear the rattle when you are out, put on your gas mark at once and get indoors as soon as you can.

Make sure that all members of your household understand the meanings of these signals.

(2) GAS MASKS

If you have already got your gask, make sure that you are keeping it safely and in good condition for immediate use. If you are moving permanently, or going away for any length of time, remember to take you gas mask with you.

SOURCE E   *Ministry of Information pamphlet.*

SOURCE G

The precautions against air raids were tested mainly in the period March to May 1942, when German Commanders ordered attacks on Britain's major historical cities (the Baedeker raids). Exeter was selected as a target and suffered extensive damage during a very heavy bombing raid on 4th May 1942.

Chris Jordan, 1986 (one of the authors of this book).

Questions

1 Explain how you might arrange Sources A–G for display in a local archive.

2 Where might you look for these sources in your town or village?

3 What story do they tell?

4 Make a note of any other information you feel ought to be included in a display panel called 'The Exeter Blitz'.

EVALUATING SOURCES

Questions

Look at the source you have been given.

1 Is this a primary or a secondary source? How do you know this?

2 Do you agree with the conclusions drawn about this source by the pupil?

3 Could anything else be said about the source which could add to its importance in the archive?

4 Could it be presented in a better way? Explain your answer.

Look carefully at Source A.

5 Could any other details about the chocolate wrapper be added if the pupils had done extra research? What might these details be? How could the research have been done?

6 Do you think the pupil is right in what he says about the reactions to cartoons as a means of conveying information? What other reactions might people have?

7 Do you think the pupil was right to redraw the cartoon instead of photocopying it? Explain your answer

Look at Source B.

8 Are the conclusions drawn from this interview as full as they could be? What else could be added about evacuees?

9 Who else could have been interviewed to improve this exhibit? How might this have been done?

Finding a good source to use in your Local Archive Project is one thing. Getting the most out of it – 'evaluating it' – is another.

Look at Sources A–C: an artefact and a cartoon; an interview and a photo; and a government advertisement.

Alongside each source is an attempt by someone to explain why they chose that source for their archive – and how they evaluated it. What do you think of their comment? Would you approach things differently? Could you do better? What are the problems evaluating different types of source?

Your teacher will suggest which sources you should examine. After you've studied the source and the comment on it, answer the questions on **Worksheet 13**.

SOURCE A

Food Shortages

ROWNTREE'S
BRUNCH
CHOCOLATE

ROWNTREE'S
BRUNCH
CHOCOLATE

ROWNTREE & Co. Ltd. YORK · ENGLAND
D/H.L. 471. H.C.

CONTROLLED PRICE 2½ᴅ EACH
PRODUCT GROUP C1

CHOCOLATE WRAPPER.

I found this tucked into a small book published by His Majesty's Stationery Office. I bought the book in a junk shop. The wrapper itself did not tell me a lot except that it is very simple, with very little writing on it and was only one layer. I thought this was because of paper shortages and the need to save printing ink. It cost 2½d (about 1p) and needed coupons to buy it because it is in Product Group C1 – the C must stand for coupon. It is

interesting because not many chocolate wrappers can have survived – during the war people would have given them in to be made into other paper.

It is really telling people that dried eggs were just as good as real eggs. Eggs were in short supply through the war so people had to make cakes and pastry using dried egg powder, a lot of which was sent over from America. It is very effective because you have to laugh at the snobby expression on the chef's face.

CARTOON.

SOURCE B

Evacuees

Interview with Mrs Bramwell who looked after two evacuees from London during the war. The interview lasted 2 hours and I tape recorded it then wrote down the parts I thought were most interesting.

INTERVIEW:

I went to the waiting room at the railway station. It was ten o'clock at night and cold and rainy. There were two little girls, sisters aged 5 and 7. They were very cold and frightened. I took them home and when I saw them in the light they were very dirty and dressed in rags. I took them to the bathroom and they had hysterics when they saw the bath— they thought I was going to drown them. The next morning I bought them new clothes even though I couldn't really afford it. They soon settled down with us and got to like having baths...

We were horrified by their bad language. We were gardening one day and one of them, Mary, dropped her fork. She shouted "Blast the f...ing b......!" I told her not to use such awful words and she got very upset and shouted "I'll tell my dad about you and he'll come and knock your bleeding block off!" It made me realise then how unhappy they were and how much they missed their parents.

Mrs. Bramwell told me about other children who were evacuated who had brown paper for underwear or were sewn into their clothes for the whole winter. Lots of the kids were dishonest and there was lots of shoplifting. They only seemed to eat fish and chips to start with.

A photo of Ann and Mary and their mother.

She was a very good person to interview because she still sees Mary and Ann. They both write to her and visit. They bring their children to stay. She had lots of photos and let me borrow this one of them and their mother. It was taken at the station on the night they left London. You can see the label on Ann with her name and address on it.

SOURCE C

Government Warnings

THESE ORDERS AFFECT YOU

Keep Off the Streets Whenever Possible

AND LISTEN FOR RAID WARNINGS

Here are some Government Orders which affect everyone from now on:—

All cinemas, theatres and other places of entertainment are to be closed immediately until further notice. In the light of experience, it may be possible to allow reopening in some areas.

Sports gatherings and all gatherings for the purposes of entertainment and amusement, whether indoor or outdoor, which attract large congregations of people, are prohibited until further notice, especially gatherings for the purpose of entertainment. All people are earnestly requested not to crowd together unnecessarily in any circumstances.

Churches will not be closed.

No hooters or sirens may be sounded except on the instruction of the police.

In the event of a threatened air raid, warnings will be given by sirens or hooters—sometimes short intermittent blasts and in others a warbling sound. Warnings may also be given by short blasts on police whistles.

When you hear these sounds, take shelter. Do not leave it until you hear the "Raiders past" signal—continuously sounded by sirens or hooters for two minutes on the same note.

If poison gas has been used, you will be warned by hand rattles. If you hear them, do not leave shelter until it has been cleared. Handbells will be rung to tell you when there is no longer any danger.

DAY SCHOOLS

All day schools in evacuation and neutral areas in England, Wales and Scotland are to be closed for lessons for at least a week. In reception areas, schools should be reopened as soon as arrangements can be completed. The precise date of the reopening will be decided on by the school authorities.

Keep off the streets as much as possible. To expose yourself unnecessarily adds to your danger. Carry your gas mask always.

Make sure you have your name and address clearly written. Have it either on an envelope or label, not on an odd piece of paper.

London Tube railways are required for traffic, and Tube stations are not available as air raid shelters.

These instructions were issued on September 3rd 1939. This was an advertisement in a special issue of the Exeter newspaper "Express and Echo". September 3rd was a Sunday.

I was interested in what people thought about all the information that was given out by the government. I read in one book that 33% of women and 11% of men did not notice the posters at all. My grandmother told me that she thought you needed a dictionary to understand most of them.

Questions

Look at Source C.

10 Has the pupil used the content of the government instructions as fully as possible? Could it, for instance, tell you more about wartime conditions than he or she has picked up? If so, what?

11 What more general points could have been made about the way the government wanted people to behave?

12 What extra points could have been made about the way that people might have reacted to this advertisement?

Look at the source you have been given.

13 Is this a useful piece of evidence? Explain your answer.

INTRODUCTION

The Universal Declaration of Human Rights, 1948

- All human beings are born free and equal.
- Everyone has the right to life, liberty and freedom from fear and violence.
- Everyone has the right to protection of the law without discrimination.
- No one shall be subjected to arbitrary arrest, detention or exile.
- Everyone has the right to a fair and public trial.
- Everyone charged with a penal offence has the right to be assumed innocent until proved guilty.
- No one shall be subjected to arbitary interference with his privacy, family, home or correspondence, nor to attacks on his reputation.
- Everyone has the right to freedom of movement within his own country and abroad.
- Everyone has the right to a nationality.
- Adult men and women have the right to marry and found a family regardless of their race or religion.
- Both men and women are entitled to equal rights within marriage and in divorce.
- Everyone has the right to own property. No one should be arbitrarily deprived of his property.
- Everyone has the right to freedom of thought, conscience and religion and the right to express their opinion both privately and publicly.
- Everyone has the right to attend meetings and joint association.
- No one should be forced to join an association.
- Everyone has the right to take part in the government of his country. Everyone has the right to work and to just and favourable conditions of employment.
- Everyone has the right to equal pay for equal work.

Summary of Human Rights

1 The right to freedom from state violence.
2 The right to food.
3 The right to organise and express belief.
4 The right to health.
5 The right to education and literacy.

World Human Rights League, 1986

Ranking of governments based on their freedom from state violence and their tolerance of dissent.

Top	%	Bottom	%
New Zealand	98	Ethiopia	13
Denmark	98	N. Korea	17
Finland	98	Iraq	19
Holland	98	Romania	20
Sweden	98	USSR	20
Norway	97	S. Africa	22
W. Germany	97	Bulgaria	23

Charles Humana, World Human Rights Guide *(1987).*

The picture story opposite reminds us of the most dreadful example of the denial of human rights in the twentieth century.

This unit of the book looks in detail at three more historical examples – from Germany and the USSR in the 1930s, and from South Africa in the 1950s. The table above shows that the denial of human rights did not stop in 1948.

The logo of the United Nations, the organisation responsible for the Universal Declaration of Human Rights.

The logo of Amnesty International, the Human Rights organisation which campaigns for the release of prisoners of conscience.

HUMAN RIGHTS

NAZI GERMANY

Introduction

The Nuremberg Laws were issued by Germany's Nazi Government in September, 1935. They were a formal statement changing the position of those German citizens who practised the Jewish faith.

Hitler's stormtroopers had begun attacks on Jewish property during the election campaigns of the early 1930s; shopwindows were smashed, slogans written on walls and synagogues attacked. At the same time, crude propaganda sheets were issued, claiming that the Jewish people were responsible for anything that seemed wrong in Weimar Germany. One example was the anti-Jewish newspaper, *Der Stürmer*, edited by Julius Streicher. Members of the Hitler Youth and other Nazi organisations were taught songs and poems that insulted Jews; Hitler's words in *Mein Kampf* were often quoted: 'By defending myself against the Jew I am fighting for the work of the Lord.'

After Hitler seized power in Germany, one of his first acts was to increase the persecution of the Jews. In September 1933, a law was passed which said that only farmers who could prove there had been no Jewish blood in their families since 1880 could inherit the land. In schools, Jewish children were forced to wear the Star of David, made to stand at the front of the class and were not allowed to take part in normal lessons. A new subject, the Science of the Races, was introduced into schools, which tried to show that the Aryans were a superior race. By 1935, notices had gone up saying that swimming pools and public parks were not to be used by Jews.

The Nuremberg Laws

Article 1: The Reich Citizenship Law

'Only a national of German or similar blood, who proves by his behaviour that he is willing and able loyally to serve the German people and Reich (state) is a citizen of the Reich.

A Jew may not be a citizen of the Reich. He has no vote . . . He may not fill public office (e.g. Mayor, Councillor, Lawyer, Teacher).

Jewish officials will be retired on December 31, 1935.'

Article 2: Law for the Protection of German Blood and German Honour

'Marriages between Jews and nationals of German or similar blood are forbidden. Jews are forbidden to hoist the Reich and national flags, and to show the Reich colours. They are on the other hand allowed to show the Jewish colours.'

Notes

1 For the purpose of these laws, a 'Jew' was held to be anybody who had one Jewish grandparent.

2 Removing the vote and right to be a citizen meant that Jews could not be protected by the law or the police.

3 'Jewish colours' (Article 2) meant the Star of David. All German Jews were required to wear a badge of identification. By July 1938, they were issued with special identity cards which they had to show on demand.

Anti-Jewish propaganda in Nazi Germany, 1933.

Crystal Night: November 1938

The Nuremberg Laws removed many basic rights and freedoms from thousands of loyal German Jews. In addition, acts of violence and thuggery continued against Jewish property and people.

On the 9 November 1938, Ernst von Rath, third Secretary of the Germany Embassy in Paris was shot and killed by a 17-year-old Polish Jew named Herschel Grynszpan. This was an act of protest by a desperate man, trying to bring attention to the way that Jews were being treated in Germany. However, the killing had the opposite effect: it released a wave of hatred in Germany which was supported by the government. Gangs roamed the streets, smashing windows and attacking synagogues, shops and private houses. Damage ran into millions of Marks, and the night of 9 November came to be known as the Kristallnacht (Crystal Night) because so much glass had been broken.

A Nazi blacklist of people using Jewish shops.

SOURCE A

The murder in Paris of Herr von Rath led Germany today to scenes of systematic plunder and destruction which have seldom had their equal in a civilised country since the Middle Ages. In every part of the Reich, synagogues were set on fire or dynamited, Jewish shops smashed and ransacked, and individual Jews arrested or hounded by bands of young Nazis through the street.

The orgy began here in the early hours of this morning with almost simultaneous outbreaks of fire in nine of the twelve synagogues of Berlin.

While these attacks were being made . . . other gangs of young men, all in plain clothes, but evidently acting according to a systematic plan, toured the streets of Berlin, smashing the windows of every Jewish shop which they encountered.

But destruction and looting did not begin in earnest until this afternoon. A large cafe in the Kurfurstendamm had been plundered of its bottles of wines and spirits and these were being gleefully thrown at what remained of the windows . . . The active participants in this display were youths and little boys of the Hitler Youth – the only uniformed body which I actually saw taking part in the destruction.

During the entire day hardly a policeman was to be seen in the streets where the 'purge' was in progress, save those few who were directing traffic. In no case, so far as can be learned, did the police dare to interfere with the demonstrators.

Berlin correspondent of The Times *10 November 1938*

Crystal Night showed how dangerous it was to live outside the protection of the law in Germany. But worse was to follow, as the Nazi 'final solution' set up death camps to eliminate all the Jews in Europe.

A SOVIET LABOUR CAMP

The years between 1935 and 1939 were a time of repression and bloodshed in the USSR. Millions of people were arrested for 'crimes against the State' and executed or sent to labour camps in remote regions. It is estimated that seven million Soviet citizens disappeared during these years.

The evidence below is taken from original sources as far as possible. It is formed from the memories of several Soviet prisoners, but it is presented as one person's story. We shall call this man Ivan.

Labour camps in the Soviet Union, 1936-66.

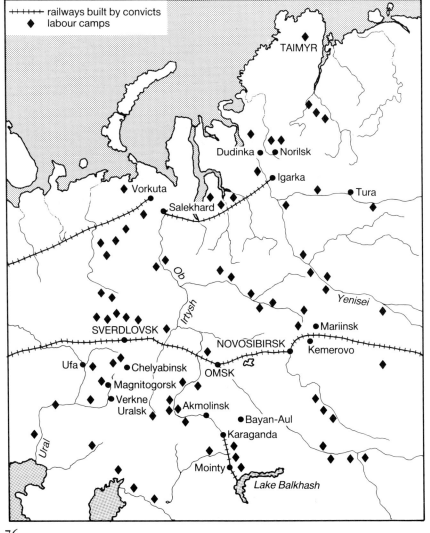

The Arrest

SOURCE A

Last year, I was at a planning conference. At the end, a tribute to Comrade Stalin was called for. Of course, everyone stood up. The small hall echoed with great applause for three, four, five minutes.

But palms were getting sore . . . However who would dare to be the first to stop? After all, NKVD men, [the secret police] were standing in the hall applauding and waiting to see who quit first! And in that obscure, small hall, unknown to the leader, the applause went on – six, seven, eight minutes! They couldn't stop now till they collapsed with heart attacks!

The director of the local paper factory, my brother (Ivan), stood with the committee. He was an independent and strong man, who after ten minutes of this insanity, suddenly sat down. And oh, a miracle took place . . . To a man, everyone else stopped dead and sat down. They had been saved! That, however, was how they discovered who the independent people were. That same night, my brother was arrested. Now I always applaud Stalin . . .

The Interrogation

Ivan was sent to an NKVD centre for questioning; 10 days later the NKVD produced a written confession whereby Ivan admitted to anti-social acts, including sabotage and treason. A fellow prisoner explained how people always signed a confession.

SOURCE B

Some idealists can be persuaded that they are no longer needed and will best serve the interests of their country by disappearing in such a manner. But most are more difficult and must be coerced, usually by destroying any hope they may ever have of obtaining justice and by threats to the lives of their wives and children. Sometimes drugs are used . . . (There was a case when a man was required to make a public confession of treason and was told that if he did not do it exactly as arranged his small son would have his head crushed in. The man apparently did not believe this. His son was picked up by the feet and his head shattered against the wall.)

The trial and the sentence

Ivan was tried for anti-Soviet activities in the town of Smolensk. The trial judge merely repeated the words of the state prosecutor, Vjshinsky at the Moscow state trial of Bukharin in summing up the case.

SOURCE C

Our whole country is awaiting and demanding one thing. The traitors and spies who were selling our country must be shot like dirty dogs. Our people are demanding one thing. Crush the accursed reptile. Time will pass. The graves of the hateful traitors will grow over with weeds and thistles. But over us, our happy country, our sun will shine, as bright and luminous as before. Over the road cleared of the scum and filth of the past, we, with our beloved leader and teacher the great Stalin at our head, will march as before onwards and upwards towards communism.

Ivan was given a sentence of 10 years' hard labour. 'I'm innocent,' he said to his NKVD guard: 'Shut up!' replied the guard. 'Of course you're not guilty. Would they have given you only 10 years if you had been?'

Ten years in the camp

Ivan was sent to a camp in the far north of Siberia, where he was set to work, clearing forests for 14 hours a day, seven days a week.

Forced labour in Russia.

SOURCE D

In the middle of a deserted, muddy plot of land, surrounded by a fence with guard towers at each corner, there stood cages, into which groups of men were put as they arrived. There the prisoners spend several days. But at night the cage barracks could not hold more than twenty per cent of the prisoners. The others wallowed in the mire, exposed to the cold and rain. They lit fires, pulling the barracks apart for wood. Now and then club-swinging guards chased the men . . . Twice a day we prisoners received one third of a litre of soup, and once a day about a kilo of bread. Drinking water was drawn from canals, ditches and puddles.

We were forced to work in temperatures of −40°F . . . Rain and snow storms were disregarded. We had to cut trees in the forests even when the snow was waist deep. Falling trees would hit the workers, who were unable to escape in the deep snow . . . At night the clothes of the men, drenched with snow or mud, were hung around the stove.

Influenza, bronchitis, pneumonia . . . and other illnesses decimated our ranks. Scurvy was widespread . . . gangrene was frequent . . . The prisoners often mutilated themselves to avoid working . . . There were many cases of suicide. In the barrack where I lived a Viennese Jew, Frischof, hanged himself. The Germans had held him in Dachau for 11 months: he had endured that imprisonment but could not stand this one.

SOUTH AFRICA: THE LAWS OF APARTHEID

Separate Amenities Act 1953: you cannot play where you like.

All shall enjoy equal human rights: the ANC Freedom Charter, 1955

"The law shall guarantee to all their right to speak, to organize, to meet together, to publish, to preach, to worship and to educate their children.

The privacy of the house from police raids should be protected by law.

All shall be free to travel without restriction from countryside to town, from province to province, and from South Africa abroad.

Pass laws, permits and all other laws restricting these freedoms shall be abolished."

Pass Laws 1952: you cannot travel where you like.

Suppression of Communism Act 1950: you cannot believe what you like.

Native (Urban Areas) Act 1945: you cannot live where you like.

Questions and Exercises

Instructions

Read the chapter on human rights (pages 72–78) carefully before completing this work section.

Exercises

1 (a) Choose either situation A or B and read the information in it. Use the information given in this unit as a starting point, plus any other research your teacher may require, to fill in **Worksheet 14** that your teacher will give you.

   (b) When you have filled in the form write about a paragraph explaining how effective you think it will be in helping your friend or relation in 1936 and then explain why you think as you do.

2 *Research*: Using your school library and any other material your teacher may give you, research into the following aspects of life in South Africa:
(a) Separate Amenities Act
(b) Pass Laws
(c) Native (Urban Areas) Act
(d) Bantustans
(e) Suppression of Communism Act
(f) African National Congress (ANC)
(g) The Sharpeville Massacre
(h) Nelson Mandela.

3 You are a Commissioner for Human Rights working for the United Nations. Write a short report in which you explain:

(a) how the system of apartheid works;
(b) how it breaks the Universal Declaration of Human Rights giving as many examples as you can;
(c) how effective the following methods might be in ending apartheid – stopping all trade with South Africa (economic sanctions) – stopping all sporting links with South Africa (sports boycott) – invasion of South Africa by the UN – support for the ANC – protesting in the UN about South African violation of human rights – doing nothing.

4 Your teacher will give you **Worksheet 15**. Reread this unit, and instructions on the Worksheet, and fill it in.

Situation A

You live in Nazi Germany during the 1930s. You are a close friend and business partner of a Jewish banker, Paul Liebowitz. Over the years you have come to like, respect and admire Herr Liebowitz, your partner. You have also been welcomed into his family on many occasions. You are not a member of the Nazi party and you do not agree with their policies. You have several relations who live abroad and one of them is a British MP. You have contacted him and he has sent you a form to fill in to keep a complete and accurate record of the persecution of your friend and his family. You will send this information to your British cousin in the hope that he will be able to do something to help – such as publishing the information in the free press and putting pressure on the German Government to stop what they are doing.

Use the information in the section on Jews in Nazi Germany to help you to draw up a detailed list of problems faced by your friend and his family. You may wish to do some extra research.

Situation B

It is 1936. You are the cousin of a Russian dissident, Irena Kalenkov. She was a history lecturer in Leningrad University but was arrested by the NKVD for 'crimes against the state' five months ago. Since then no one in her family has been able to contact her although you all suspect that she has been sent to a labour camp in Siberia.

Irena is 53 and not in good health. She was an important figure in the Revolution of 1917 and became one of Lenin's secretaries. She has been quite outspoken in her criticism of the present agricultural reforms, especially in connection with the deportation of the kulaks.

You have a relation who emigrated to the USA in 1900 and is now a member of the US Government. You have managed to smuggle a message to him and he has sent you and official form to fill in with details of Irena's case.

Use the information in the section on the Russian dissident, Ivan as a guideline to help you fill in the form about Irena. You may wish to do some extra research.

Exercises

Look carefully at the picture story on page 73.

1 Re-tell the story in your own words. Draw one more picture to show a different ending to the story.

2 Do you feel sorry for any of the characters in the story? Explain your answer.

3 What does this story tell you about human rights?

4 Find out about the final solution (1942-45) employed by the Nazis. What did the Nazis hope to achieve?

5 Answer the final question for the character – 'My God, how did it come to this?'

6 Produce a bar chart, map, league table or any other representation to show the figures for human rights shown on page 72. Underneath your table/chart, write the answers to the following questions:
(a) What does this chart show?
(b) How accurate is it?
(c) Does it surprise you?
(d) Where do you feel the United Kingdom would be positioned in your chart?
(e) Why are league tables like this published?

7 Find out any current news story (from a newspaper, magazine or TV/radio news) concerned with human rights. Write a paragraph explaining:
(a) what the story was;
(b) how it was treated by the news media;
(c) what was the point of the story;
(d) what your opinion is of the treatment of the story by the media.

1900–45

Background 1900–1919

In 1900, India was one of the most important countries in the British Empire. The population of over 300 million Indians was ruled by a few thousand British officials. The people had many different languages and religions, but the majority were Hindus. The largest minority were Muslims.

As early as 1885, middle-class Indians who were dissatisfied with British rule began to demand more power. They held the first Indian Congress (which later developed into a political party) demanding social reforms and better opportunities for educated Indians. The Congress won some reforms but these only applied to Hindus. So in 1906, the Muslims formed the Muslim League to demand similar reforms for their people.

World War 1

During World War 1, hundreds of thousands of Indian troops fought for the British Empire. Indian demands for independence became louder and in 1917, the British government agreed that some time after the war, India should become a self-governing country.

Events at the end of the war helped the Indian cause in several ways. The American President Wilson's point concerning national self-determination laid down in the Treaty of Versailles, was a powerful argument in support of Indian independence and the break-up of the Austro-Hungarian Empire seemed to show that Empires could be dismantled peacefully. In addition, the Russian revolution was a warning to the British of how an unpopular government could be violently overthrown.

1919–39

A new form of government was set up consisting of a type of Parliament called the Central Legislative Assembly. However, the Assembly was dominated by Indian princes, who mainly supported British rule and were not interested in giving power to the Indian people. Very few Indians (about five million) were able to vote, because they had to own a certain amount of property to qualify. Many of the important powers, such as control of the police, were still directly in the hands of the King's Representative, of the British Viceroy.

The Indians continued to protest and in 1919 a peaceful demonstration at Amritsar was broken up by British troops who opened fire, killing about 380 people and wounding over 1200.

Mohandas Karamchand Gandhi

Gandhi was born in 1869. He studied at London University and qualified as a barrister. He then went to work in South Africa and led opposition to the racial laws. He started a unit of the Indian Red Cross during the Boer War. On returning to India in 1914, he set up an Indian ambulance corps.

Gandhi became the leader of the nationalist movement in India. He earned the title 'Mahatma' which means 'great soul'.

Gandhi's ideas

Gandhi believed that India should be independent from British rule, and that Muslims and Hindus should be equal. He thought that independence should be achieved by non-violent methods (passive resistance). Passive resistance had three elements: civil disobedience, refusing to buy British goods and publicising India's struggle for independence. *Civil disobedience* included refusing to obey unfair laws and refusing to pay unfair taxes. (He led Indians on a march to the sea to distill their own salt from sea water to avoid paying a salt tax.) He supported

Gandhi in London.

the *boycotting of (refusing to buy) British goods* and set up Indian home industries (e.g. spinning and weaving in villages). He also encouraged *mass demonstrations and publicity* to force the British to leave India.

Gandhi was sent to prison several times, but many Indians looked on him as their leader. However, by 1939, there had been no agreement about Indian independence and many Muslims had begun to demand a separate state from the Hindus.

World War 2

In 1939, the Viceroy of India declared war on Germany without consulting the Indians. Congress demanded independence in return for Indian help in the war. When the British only promised 'Dominion status', the Congress opposed the war effort and demanded that the British should 'quit India'. There were demonstrations and riots during which many leaders, including Gandhi, were arrested. A few Hindus angry at the British went to fight for the Japanese who were planning to invade India. The Muslims agreed to help but in return demanded a separate Muslim state called Pakistan. By the end of the war the British government realised that it could no longer control the discontented Indians and decided to give India independence.

SOURCE A

British officer in India, 1870.

SOURCE B

We believe that it is the right of the Indian people to have freedom . . . India has been ruined economically . . . village industries have been destroyed . . . We hold it to be a crime against man and God to submit any longer to a rule that has caused this disaster to our country . . . We recognise however, that the most effective way of gaining our freedom is not through violence.

Declaration of Independence by the Congress Party, 1930.

SOURCE C

Gandhi leading the Salt March.

SOURCE D

Gandhi and his peasants marched down to the sea carrying pots and pans which they filled with sea water. As night fell, great fires were lit on the sea shore and the water was boiled until only salt remained.

SOURCE E

Gandhi giving a demonstration of spinning.

SOURCE F

I have not become His Majesty's First Minister in order to preside over the dissolution of the British Empire.

Winston Churchill, 1941.

SOURCE G

If you are in a place where you are not wanted and where you have not got the force to squash those who do not want you, the only thing to do is to come out.

Hugh Dalton, member of the Labour Government, 1945.

Questions

1 Explain the two reasons given by the Congress Party in Source B for wanting the British to leave India.

2 Explain the principle of 'passive resistance' (referred to in Source B) and describe three methods based on this principle used by Gandhi and his followers to get the British to 'quit India'.

3 Why did Gandhi lead a march to the sea, as described in Source D and as shown in Source C?

4 Why was Gandhi so often shown spinning thread (Source E)?

5 How had the British government's attitude to India changed between 1941 and 1945 according to Sources F and G?

6 Give three reasons why this change had occurred.

THE FUTURE OF INDIA

Gandhi visiting political prisoners.

In 1947, Lord Louis Mountbatten was sent to India to be Viceroy in charge of the settlement. He was a relative of the king and had been Supreme Commander of the Allied Forces in South East Asia during the war.

Clement Attlee was the leader of the new Labour Government which came to power in 1945. He had decided that India should become independent.

Mohammed Ali Jinnah was the leader of the Muslim League. He wanted the Muslims to have their own separate country – Pakistan – and had decided that he would no longer follow peaceful methods to get what he wanted. He encouraged local leaders to use violence to show their opposition to Congress.

Jawaharlal Nehru was the leader of Congress. He wanted a united India with Muslims and Hindus working together. However, many other members of Congress did not want the Muslims to be equal nor did they want the Muslims to have their own independent state. Many members of Congress feared and hated the Muslim League.

1945–48

In 1945, a new Labour Government came to power in Britain. Its leader, Clement Attlee, promised independence to India. While the discussions went on there were racial and religious riots all over India which led to massacres of Hindus, Sikhs and Muslims. Each group tried to make sure that any new settlement did not result in them being controlled by another group. Racial tension and bitterness increased.

Mountbatten's decision

You are an adviser to Mountbatten. You have been given the task of drawing up proposals for giving India independence. Use the map and the information below to help you.

1 Look at the following policy options and write down the advantages and disadvantages of each policy and what problems each may cause.

2 Explain which groups may object to or support each proposal and why. The groups are Hindus, Sikhs, Muslims, Congress, Muslim League and the British government.

3 Explain which individuals may object to or support each proposal and why.

4 Prepare a short speech explaining which of the proposals you will recommend to Mountbatten and why you consider it to be the best option. Explain which people or groups will have to be persuaded to change their minds in order for your policy to be adopted and how you will set about doing this.

Proposal A

Refuse to give India independence. Racial and religious riots prove that India is not yet ready for self-government.

Proposal B

Offer India complete independence in June 1948 when all British troops will pull out. Make no effort to settle disagreements between the different groups of Indians but just let them come to their own arrangements.

Proposal C

Partition India. This means the country will be divided to give the Muslims and the Hindus their own states – India and Pakistan. Partition into two separate countries will cause problems such as the division of the Civil Service and Army which at present contain Indians of all religions; and division of the railway system and irrigation schemes which would cross the boundaries of any new states created.

Proposal D

Offer India immediate 'Dominion status' (i.e. self-government within the British Empire equal to all other countries in the Empire, united through loyalty to the British Crown and membership of the British Commonwealth). India will not be partitioned but will become a federal state with one central government and several provincial governments. Provinces will be given a good deal of power so that Muslim provinces can have a strong say in the federal government. Muslim provinces will be given the right to unite to form Muslim Unions within the federal government. All Muslim members of the central government will be chosen by the Muslim League.

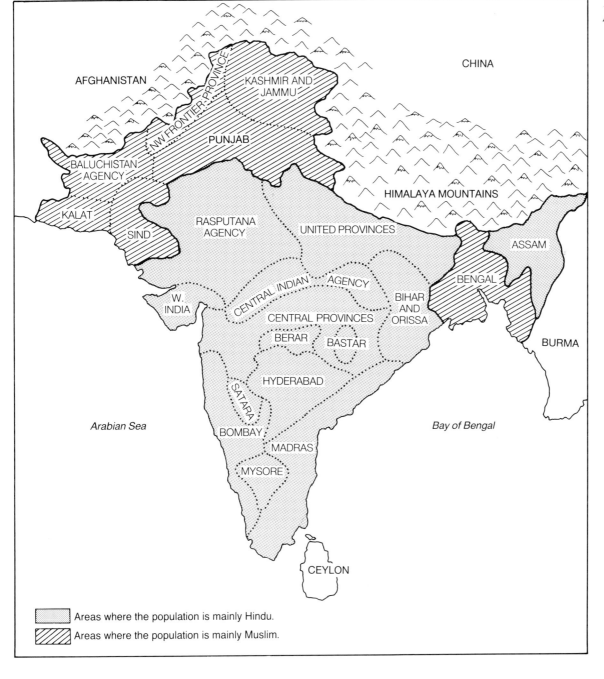

Muslim and Hindu population of India, 1948.

Areas where the population is mainly Hindu.

Areas where the population is mainly Muslim.

PARTITION

Mountbatten's Decision Part B:

Mountbatten seems to favour partition – that is the creation of a mainly Hindu state of India and a mainly Muslim state of Pakistan.

Instructions

Mountbatten has told you to prepare a feasibility study to see how partition would work.

1 You must use the map opposite and the information about the 35 provinces in **Resource G** to decide the shape of the new countries of Pakistan and India. In each case choose one of the options available and fill it in on **Worksheet 17**. Remember you must take particular notice of religion and also consider whether the country will be large enough and have strong enough frontiers to survive.

The map opposite shows the main states of India and Pakistan. NB: some of these states were created after the partition, but have been included to simplify the partition exercise. Use this map to trace a final map of India after partition.

2 Once you have done this you must draw out the new map of India and Pakistan marking on it *only* the outlines of the two new countries. Mark their capital cities.

3 You must then make a list of areas which are likely to cause problems to the new governments of India and Pakistan. Explain in each case what this trouble is likely to be (this may be riots, refugees, war etc.) and what the Indian and Pakistan governments are likely to do about them.

A demonstration by the Muslim League in Lahore.

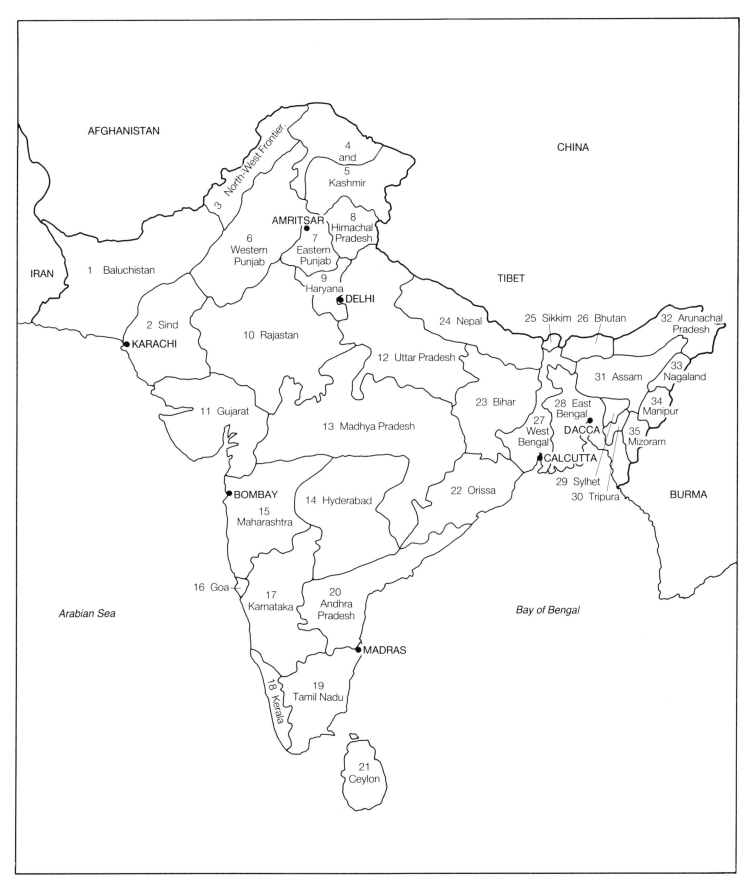

AFGHANISTAN

CHINA

3 North-West Frontier

4 and

5 Kashmir

AMRITSAR

8 Himachal Pradesh

6 Western Punjab

7 Eastern Punjab

IRAN

1 Baluchistan

9 Haryana

DELHI

TIBET

2 Sind

24 Nepal

25 Sikkim 26 Bhutan

32 Arunachal Pradesh

KARACHI

10 Rajastan

12 Uttar Pradesh

31 Assam

33 Nagaland

11 Gujarat

13 Madhya Pradesh

23 Bihar

28 East Bengal

34 Manipur

27 West Bengal

DACCA

35 Mizoram

CALCUTTA

BOMBAY

14 Hyderabad

22 Orissa

29 Sylhet

15 Maharashtra

30 Tripura

BURMA

16 Goa

17 Karnataka

20 Andhra Pradesh

Arabian Sea

Bay of Bengal

MADRAS

18 Kerala

19 Tamil Nadu

21 Ceylon

INDIA AFTER INDEPENDENCE

Drought.

On 15 August 1947, India became independent. It was the world's largest democracy with over 170 million voters. Nehru became the first Prime Minister, leading a Congress government until his death in 1964. He was opposed both by Hindu traditionalists, who did not agree with policies which attacked their religious beliefs, and by the Untouchables, the lowest Hindu social caste. Gandhi was assassinated by a Hindu fanatic in 1948.

Bullock cart.

Hand planting.

An untouchable sweeping the street.

Problems faced by India

Poverty

Most Indians lived below the poverty line. Many died of starvation each day.

Religion

The Hindu religion caused several problems which made rapid economic progress difficult.

The Caste system. Hindu society has a built-in class structure called the caste system. A person's status, job and marriage prospects are all governed by which caste he or she is born into. There are four main castes, although these in turn are sub-divided into dozens of others. They are Brahmins (priests), Kshatriyas (warriors), Vaishyas (merchants and landowners) and Sudras (labourers). Outside the caste system are the Harijans (untouchables) who are only allowed to do the worst jobs such as moving rubbish.

The caste system created great differences in wealth among Indians and also made it hard to run a modern state with opportunities for all. Women were also regarded as inferior.

Fate. The Hindu religion teaches its followers to accept their fate. This made it hard to raise living standards.

Beliefs. Certain beliefs made progress difficult in certain areas. For example, the cow is a sacred animal which cannot be eaten; however, in times of famine the cow might end up better fed than the people.

Population

In 1947, there were 400 million Indians. The population rose by about 2% per year after that. This tended to wipe out any increases in agricultural production, leading to more poverty and starvation. Overcrowding in cities led to epidemic diseases.

Farming

Indians were unable to produce enough food to feed themselves. The climate caused constant problems with many droughts. Irrigation schemes were expensive. As a result there were frequent famines and India was forced to import food which could be very expensive. The problem was made worse by the rapidly rising population which constantly demanded more food.

Dam on the Matalila Reservoir.

Industry

Industry was not very modern. Less than 0.5% of the population worked in industry. There were few modern machines or factories. Modernisation meant importing expensive machinery from the west. India had few ways of earning the money to pay for these imports.

Illiteracy

Over 85% of children left school before the age of 11, and many, especially girls, didn't go to school at all. So a large proportion of the population was unable to read or write. This made modernisation of industry and agriculture very difficult.

Corruption

The pace of the bureaucracy was painfully slow. In order to get things done at a reasonable speed it was often necessary to resort to bribery.

The Five Year Plan

It was decided that in order to modernise India a series of three Five Year Plans should be introduced to tackle India's problems, which are summarised below.

The main problems

India has a large population which must be fed. India cannot feed this population at the moment. Agriculture is badly affected by frequent droughts. Methods of production depend on hand and buffalo power.

India has large natural resources (iron, coal, oil, minerals). Many of these resources are in remote parts of India.

India is short of power. Many villages and towns do not have electricity.

There is a great shortage of houses. In large cities like Calcutta, hundreds of thousands of people live on the pavements.

One third of the population works and supports the remaining two-thirds which does not because they are small children or old people.

The population is rising too fast. Even huge increases in food production will only just feed the people who are being born.

Industry is mainly based in the home (spinning, weaving, handicrafts, etc). There is little money available to buy the expensive foreign machinery needed to modernise Indian industry.

Instructions

You are an economic adviser to the government. Your task is to decide what the priorities should be in each Five Year Plan. Your teacher will give you **Worksheet 18** to fill in and **Resource H** to help you.

India had a plentiful supply of cheap labour.

Travelling by train in India.

Questions

1 What were India's main problems in 1948?

2 Explain why India's economic development was very fast in the first eight years after 1948 and then slowed down dramatically.

3 Explain how a huge and poor population could be an advantage to Indian economic development. Explain how it could be a disadvantage.

SUPERPOWER RIVALRY: THE CUBAN CRISIS

SOURCE A   *Fidel Castro.*

SOURCE B   *Castro and his supporters in Havana.*

Cuba is an island lying 160 kilometres off the south-eastern coast of the USA. It was freed from Spanish rule and became a republic in 1898. For the next 60 years it was ruled by several dictators who received aid and support from the USA.

In 1933, a sergeant in the Cuban army, Fulgencio Batista, seized power. He was a corrupt and brutal dictator who organised a reign of terror between 1952 and 1958, executing his enemies and stealing government money. By 1956 he had made Cuba bankrupt.

In 1956, 40% of Cubans were illiterate and very poor although a few (about 2% of the population) were very rich and powerful, owning 50% of the land.

American policy towards Cuba

The American government backed any Cuban government as long as it supported the USA. In 1956, the USA owned a large military base on Cuba and had a large stake in the Cuban economy. American businessmen owned most of Cuba's oil, mines, cattle ranches and public utilities as well as 50% of its railways. Cuba's most important export was sugar and the USA bought most of its harvest every year.

Cuban Revolution

In December 1956, Fidel Castro landed in Cuba and began a revolution to overthrow Batista. Many poor Cubans joined his guerilla band fighting in the mountains. By January 1959 Castro's forces had overthrown the government. Batista and his supporters fled, many going to the USA.

Questions

Look at the map on this page.

1 Why would events on Cuba be important to the USA in the following ways:
(a) economically;
(b) politically;
(c) historically;
(d) militarily?

Look at the photographs on page 88.

2(a) Briefly explain the events leading up to the scene shown in Source B.
(b) Comment on the dress and appearance of Castro's supporters. Why do they look like this?
(c) Do you think the American government will want to support Castro as leader of Cuba after 1959? Give your reasons.

THE CUBAN CRISIS GAME

Instructions for the game

1 Your teacher will divide you into groups.

2 Half of each group will play the part of the Russian Premier, Nikita Khrushchev, and his advisers and the other half will play the part of the American Presidents, Dwight D. Eisenhower and John F. Kennedy, and their advisers.

3 Your teacher will give you a briefing sheet (**Resource I**) which states your country's aims. Your task is to achieve these aims. You do this by studying the situation and deciding which action or actions you will take in each of the rounds. There are five rounds.

4 The actions you can take are shown on the flowcharts (**Resources J and K**) which your teacher will give you. The Americans use the USA flowchart and the Russians use the USSR flowchart.

5 Place a token (coin or similar) on the start box. You may take any of the actions shown in the boxes for the round being played, provided you obey three simple rules. These are:

(i) You must move your token along the lines shown into an action box. You cannot jump from box to box.

(ii) You must move your token sideways or down the page. You cannot move your token upwards nor can you move along the same line more than once. You cannot reverse your progress.

(iii) If you pass through a box, you must make the move in that box.

6 The flowcharts are quite complicated. You are advised to consider *only* those actions available for the round you are playing. However, it is worth looking ahead, as an action you take in an early round could affect actions you take in later rounds.

7 As each round starts your teacher will give you a briefing sheet (**Resource L**) containing a summary of the world news for that round and a detailed explanation of the action shown in the action boxes for that round. Sometimes there will be extra material to consider.

8 Some of the actions are secret. You should not reveal these to your opponents.

9 You may look at your opponents' flowchart to help you.

10 You have two aims in the game:
(a) to achieve the two aims of your country as shown on your briefing sheet, and
(b) to avoid nuclear war.

However, in order to achieve your aims you may have to take the world to the brink of nuclear war. You must decide when, or if, you pull back from nuclear war.

11 Short periods of discussion will be allowed during each round. You should use these to decide on your plans and negotiate with your opponents. Any promises you make during discussion periods are not binding.

12 When you have decided on your actions, enter them on the Score Sheet (**Worksheet 20**) which your teacher will give you.

13 Each action is numbered for reference and also carries a point score. This point score represents the danger of the action. Dangerous moves, with high risks, which will increase the likelihood of nuclear war, carry high scores. Low risk moves, that decrease world tension and lower the likelihood of nuclear war, carry low scores.

14 At the end of each round, when all moves have been made, your teacher will give out the scores. You must add up the points score of all your actions. You then *add* your points score to your opponents'.

15 If at any time the total score is greater than 60, that is 61 or over, nuclear war has broken out between Russia and the USA, and the world is destroyed in a nuclear holocaust.

16 At the end of each round you will be asked to make a press statement to the world (a short speech). In this you will anounce which actions you have taken and, if you want, you can explain why you have taken these actions. You do not have to reveal secret actions you take at this stage but you should try to present your actions in a positive light to swing world opinion behind you.

17 At the end of round 5 all groups will reach an 'Outcome' and the game ends.

18 You will then be asked to look at what actually happened and compare the results of your game with the reality.

Exercises

Answer one or both of these questions.

1 You are the photo researcher for the *New York Times*. You have to select one photo for the edition of 26 October 1962, which will appear on the front page next to an article about the Cuban Crisis.

These photographs are sources A, B and C. You must choose one.
(a) Write a comment on each of the photographs saying whether you think it is the right one for your newspaper.
(b) Explain which you will choose and why.
(c) Would Mr Kennedy have approved of your choice? Give reasons for your answer.
(d) Is the newspaper likely to give a full and true account of the Cuban Crisis? Explain your answer.

2 You are the photo researcher for *Pravda*. You have to select one photo for the edition of 26 October 1962, which will appear on the front page next to an article about the Cuban Crisis.

These photographs are sources A, B and C. You must choose one.
(a) Write a comment on each of the photographs saying whether you think it is the right one for your newspaper.
(b) Explain which you will choose and why.
(c) Would Mr Khrushchev have approved of your choice? Give reasons for your answer.
(d) Is the newspaper likely to give a full and true account of the Cuban Crisis? Explain your answer.

SOURCE A *Khrushchev.*

SOURCE B *Khrushchev.*

SOURCE C *Kennedy.*

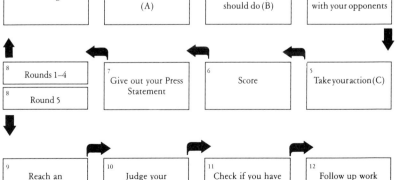

Summary of Cuban Crisis Game

1 Read Briefing Sheet	2 Listen to World News (A)	3 Decide what you should do (B)	4 Discuss the situation with your opponents
8 Rounds 1–4 / 8 Round 5	7 Give out your Press Statement	6 Score	5 Take your action (C)
9 Reach an 'Outcome'	10 Judge your performance	11 Check if you have achieved your aims	12 Follow up work

CUBAN CRISIS EXERCISES

SOURCE A

Exercises

1 Complete the following statements:
(a) In playing the game I . . .
(b) Three things I remember from the game are . . .
(c) Two things I did well during the game were . . .
(d) Two things I did badly were . . .
(e) The main thing I learnt from the game was . . .

2 Using your flowchart, action sheet, score sheet and the timeline to help you, explain your aims, actions and your progress in the Cuban Crisis game.

3 What was the outcome of your actions? How did this compare with the outcome of the real Crisis? Explain any differences there were.

4 Comment on the performance of the following people or groups during the real Crisis:
(a) Premier Khrushchev
(b) President Kennedy
(c) the CIA.

5 It is autumn 1962. You are an adviser to President John F. Kennedy. You have just been given Source A which shows that the Russians are building missile sites in Cuba. Look at the following actions which you could advise President Kennedy to take. In each case explain the *advantages* and *disadvantages* of each policy. Copy the table and fill it in – yours will be much bigger.

Policy	Advantages	Disadvantages
Do nothing.		
Bomb Cuba.		
Invade Cuba.		
Attack the USSR.		
Blockade Cuba.		
Offer to withdraw American missiles based in Turkey if the USSR withdraws its missiles from Cuba.		
Appeal to the UN for help.		

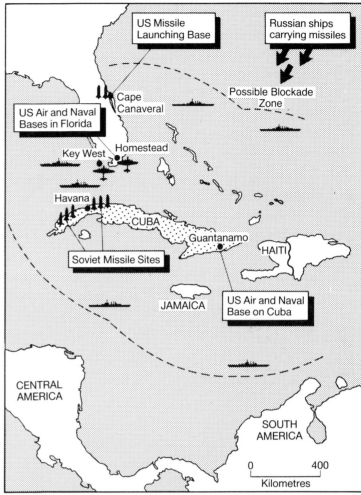

6 Use the pictures on this page to help you write an account of the Cuban Crisis.

UNDERSTANDING WHAT HAPPENED

Questions

Look at Sources A and B.

1 Explain the circumstances which led to these two remarks being made.

Look at Sources C and D.

2 Which of these two views comes closest to your own views of the Cuban Crisis? Explain why you think as you do.

Look at Sources E and F.

3 (a) Give reasons why General Lemay might have expressed this opinion.

(b) What does Kennedy imply might have been the result of following General Lemay's policy?

(c) Why did Kennedy decide not to follow General Lemay's policy?

(d) Why might an historian have reason to criticise Source F as a piece of historical evidence?

Look at Source G.

4 (a) What did Vassilij mean by this?

(b) How do you think Soviet policy changed as a result of the Cuban Crisis?

Look at Source H.

5 (a) Explain how each of these points helped to solve the Cuban Crisis.

(b) Suggest other reasons which influenced the outcome of the Cuban Crisis.

Instructions

Read the Timeline which your teacher will give you. Then read the Sources and answer the questions.

SOURCE A

We're eyeball to eyeball and I think the other fellow just blinked.

American Secretary of State Dean Rusk, 24 October 1962.

SOURCE B

The American paper tiger has atomic teeth.

Premier Khrushchev, 12 December 1962, to the Supreme Soviet.

SOURCE C

I just don't think there was any other choice.

Robert Kennedy after the crisis when talking of the actions taken by his brother, President John F. Kennedy.

SOURCE D

America was 'too eager to liquidate this thing – so long as we had the thumbscrews on Khrushchev, we should have given it another turn every day'.

American ex-Secretary of State Dean Acheson.

SOURCE E

If we had invaded Cuba I am sure the Soviets would have acted. They would have to, just as we would, too. I think there are certain compulsions on any major power.

President Kennedy after the Cuban Crisis.

SOURCE F

We attack Monday in any case.

Rumoured to have been said by General Curtis Lemay of US Strategic Air Command, 28 October 1962.

SOURCE M

SOURCE G

And this is the last time the United States will be able to do that to the Soviet Union.

Deputy Foreign Minister Vassilij when agreeing to remove Russian bombers from Cuba.

SOURCE H

President Kennedy said the Cuban Crisis had three distinctive features:
1 The Crisis took place in an area of traditional American interest.
2 The USA had a massive military superiority in the Caribbean.
3 Once the American photographs of the missile sites had been shown in the UN, the Russians could not persuade the world of their innocence.

A modern historian.

SOURCE I

The Cuban Crisis was a less terrifying experience for Khrushchev than for Kennedy, because it was lack of knowledge about the former's motives that had mainly caused such alarm in Washington. For Khrushchev, who had never meant to go to war, the main problem once he had realised his basic miscalculation was to prevent any damage to his own and Soviet standing.

From Khrushchev by Mark Frankland (1966).

Look at Source M.

1 What type of historical source is this?

2 Who are the two men shown in the picture?

3 What are they sitting on? How do you know this?

4 What are the men doing with their right hands? Why are they doing this?

5 What are the two men doing with their left hands? Why are they doing this?

6 What event is Source M supposed to represent?

7 Is Source M an accurate representation of the event? Explain your answer.

8 Is Source M an effective representation of the event? Explain your answer.

SOURCE J

The President's crucial achievement...was to make Khrushchev understand that he must withdraw by showing him the nuclear abyss to the edge of which he had blundered and pointing the way back without disgrace.

From The Missiles of October by the American historian Elie Abel.

SOURCE K

I think he did it because of the Bay of Pigs. I think he thought that anyone who was so young and inexperienced as to get into that mess could be taken; and anyone who got into it and didn't see it through, had no guts. So he just beat the hell out of me... If he thinks I'm inexperienced and have no guts, until we remove those ideas we won't get anywhere with him.

Kennedy, of Khrushchev after the Vienna Summit meeting of 1961, explaining the Russian leader's threatening attitude at the Summit.

SOURCE L

During the week of the Cuban Crisis Premier Khrushchev made several public appearances in Moscow, giving an interview to an important American businessman, chatting with an American singer at the Bolshoi Theatre and going to the ballet.

From Khrushchev by Mark Frankland (1966).

Questions

Look at Sources I and J.

6 (a) What common point are both these writers making about Mr Khrushchev?
(b) These two writers give different reasons for the withdrawal of the USSR from the Cuban Crisis. Explain their two different points of view.
(c) Why do they have different points of view?

Look at Source K.

7 (a) Does this statement help to explain Mr Khruschev's behaviour before, during or after the Cuban Crisis? Explain your answer.
(b) Does this statement help to explain President Kennedy's behaviour during the Cuban Crisis?

Look at Source L.

8 (a) Can you suggest why he did this?
(b) Do the facts in Source L tend to support the opinions expressed in Source I or the opinions expressed in Source J? Give your reasons.

Use all the sources on these pages plus the material used in the Cuban Crisis game.

9 Do these sources give a balanced view of the Cuban Crisis? Explain your answer.

10 Do these sources give a complete view of the Cuban Crisis? Explain your answer.

11 Write an essay describing the causes, events and results of the Cuban Crisis.